"At a time when our society fee
White's *Contact: The Shaping Power of Intentional Interaction* makes a compelling case from both the Bible and research that relationships with those who are different from ourselves are vital to developing empathy and mutual understanding. It's an important message for the Church today."

Matthew Soerens
U.S. Director of Church Mobilization &
Advocacy, World Relief; Coauthor of *Welcoming the Stranger:*
Justice, Compassion, and Truth in the Immigration Debate

"Into our deeply fractured and polarized culture wars, which are tearing apart our national unity and damaging the credibility of the church, comes this truly helpful and timely book by Tyler White. *Contact* addresses many of the core problems we face in a globalized and over-wired world of competing 'truth' ghettos, out of touch with each other. He provides not only analysis to help us understand how we got here, but practical steps toward deeper engagement and correction. While his work is helpful for those in a secular environment, it is especially significant for followers of Jesus who want to follow the Prince of Peace in healing and uniting all people made in God's image. I am eager to see this book in publication so that I can recommend it to every church leader I know."

Dan Bouchelle, DMin
President, Mission Resource Network

"*Contact* is a necessary read for America. At a time in our nation where healthy dialogue and discourse are rare, White's text provides a clear and pragmatic approach forward. Not only does *Contact* identify the root causes of conversation failure, it offers examples and illustrations from sacred and secular environments. This is a transformative and compelling read that speaks to all peoples regardless of gender, race, religion, political ideology, or socioeconomic status. *Contact* equips those who want discourse to improve with the necessary tools to make the theoretical possible."

Joshua Jackson
Lead Minister, Rural Hill Church of Christ

"I remember the first time I heard the term 'contact theory.' I felt the truth of this simple-yet-profound idea in my own experience working in a refugee community. I wanted to dig in and know more. And I wanted others, especially the community of those who follow Jesus, to understand how important it is to move intentionally toward people who are different from us. What I wanted was a book like the one Tyler White has written, a book that both inspires and instructs, that challenges and creates a path to meet that challenge. *Contact* is a much-needed encouragement for our time."

Kitti Murray
Founder and CEO, Refuge Coffee Co.

"In a day and age where division is heightening due to disagreements on a plethora of issues, Tyler does a fantastic job of giving us a blueprint on the importance of being in contact with others from different backgrounds and life experiences—with others who might look, think, and act differently than we do. This is a timely book that all fellow Christians need to read."

Rondell Treviño
Founder and Director, The Immigration Coalition

"Are you weary of our current climate of polarization and fear? This book is a must read. With a potent mixture of scriptural encouragement, historical background, social science research, case studies, and insights from personal experience, White calls the Church to lay aside knee-jerk stereotypes in order to engage in humble listening across cultural, political, and generational divides in order to develop true unity in diversity."

Jessica Udall
Author of *Loving the Stranger;*
Founder of LovingTheStrangerBlog.com

"*Contact* is jam-packed with intriguing history (some you will recognize—some you may discover here for the first time) and narratives about the impact of human contact. This book comes at an important time in our timeline of humanity as we grasp the impact of social media and grapple with what it means to be truly connected."

Justin Velten, PhD
President, Go Culture International

CONTACT

THE SHAPING POWER OF INTENTIONAL INTERACTION

TYLER WHITE

Deep River
B O O K S

To my parents. You listen well and love even better. Thank you for always being a great example of what it means to serve others. With love and gratitude.

CONTENTS

INTRODUCTION

Running for Mayor, Making Friends, and Influencing People

Lee Jenkins, founder and pastor of Eagles Nest Church, and also a businessman in Roswell, GA, ran for mayor of Roswell in 2017. Roswell is an affluent suburb in the North Atlanta metro area; the population estimate in 2017 was about 95,000. The estimated median household income of Roswell in 2017 was $82,743, and the demographic makeup 63.3 percent Caucasian.[1] As an African American, Lee's attempt at winning a mayoral race in a predominantly white city would prove challenging.

As Lee's campaign began to flourish and his platform of leadership and unity began to gain attention, voices opposing him and his message began to intensify. Lee could have simply avoided them or used his public platform to get the upper hand, but he chose a different approach. Once he found out about this local, organized opposition, he decided he wanted to meet with them. His campaign team pushed back and discouraged him from the meeting, but Lee insisted that they deserved the chance to get to know and understand him.

Eventually, Lee was able to get a meeting with this group that opposed him. He was able to share about himself, his character, and his vision for Roswell. Long story short: at the end of the meeting, these same community leaders who had opposed him became advocates and supporters of his campaign!

This is a powerful story of how contact works. Lee was able to come in contact with those who resisted his candidacy and completely overhaul their perception of him. These community leaders didn't know who Lee was as a real person, but after getting to know him and coming in contact with him, they were able to gain an understanding that defeated any generalizations or prejudice they may have had against him.

There are two sides to this story. One is that Lee insisted on meeting these community leaders. But the other side is that these leaders also had to be open to accepting the meeting.

Sometimes God is putting contact moments right in front of us; all we have to do is answer the call to embrace them and be open to learn from them. This book will examine how valuing and recognizing the importance of intentional interactions and personal relationships, and perspectives of people from different backgrounds and life experiences than your own, can bring to fruition a deeper understanding of what it means to love others and to love God.

A Gathering of Observations

The ideas and examples introduced in this book are a gathering of observations applied upon a biblical and theological foundation that I have been linking together for some time now. Throughout some of my graduate school research, I developed some research questions that I didn't fully get a chance to answer and wanted to dive into more deeply. The ideas and examples in this book are a product of trying to answer those questions by examining the research and stories that already exist.

I began simply by noticing and observing how divergent people's perspectives were . . . about anything really. It seemed to me that a lot of us were living in two completely different worlds sometimes—likely a product of our cultural backgrounds and the way we gather and interpret information. I understand that this is nothing new. The history of the entire world is laced with events that have brought separation among people for as long as we have lived. Prejudice, discrimination, violence, and more are all interconnecting elements that continue to feed into the marred relationships that individuals, groups, cultures, and nations continue to have with each other.

However, I believe now is a pivotal moment in history. We need to begin to truly understand people and learn to understand, respect, and love people and their cultural backgrounds and life experiences or other differences that historically have served as separators. Even (especially) in Christendom, we have often allowed fear, stereotypes, generalizations, and prejudice to infiltrate our belief systems, blocking our understanding and blinding us from respecting people and engaging in dignified dialogue about various issues.

My own personal experiences have contributed to the writing of this book. Throughout my journey, I learned that having intentional relationships with people from different backgrounds helped me understand their perspective on certain topics. I began looking at friends and others, how they developed relationships with those different from themselves on certain levels, and how the overall understanding of the group that person was a part of began to change—generalizations decreased and perspectives increased. It seemed that the people who were spending time with people and groups from different backgrounds than themselves were the ones who were the most understanding and the most accepting of differences. On the contrary, it seemed that the people who only spent time with other people from the same background were the ones who were usually resistant to understanding and acceptance of differences. My anecdotal observations led me to a hypothesis: personal and intentional relationships develop perspective and understanding, in turn reducing negative generalizations we easily and often make about people.

Sounds simple, right? But you would be surprised how slow we humans are to apply such a simple idea to our lives. I began to search for research on this specific topic to see what, if anything, existed. I came across *The Nature of Prejudice,* released in 1954 by a psychologist named Gordon Allport, which thoroughly examined various levels of prejudice from a variety of angles, and its causes and effects. Allport's research resulted in a hypothesis called *contact hypothesis,* or *contact theory.* With this theory, Allport introduced, as a product of his research, how humans and groups can reduce their prejudice toward each other, especially with majority and minority groups. Contact theory posited that as people spend time with each other and get to know each other, their value of each other increases. Allport's research has been thoroughly tested by various scholars who have evidenced positive results of contact theory, more of which will be examined later.

I began to wonder how the seemingly simple idea of building intentional relationships with people who are different from ourselves can help us understand each other better, love each other more deeply, and bring dignified dialogue to the table. I wondered how Christians have applied this in our approaches to relationships, or at least how we could lead the way in building these relationships with people from different backgrounds. As my research and thoughts progressed on this topic, I realized that Christians were struggling to take this simple idea into account—and in reality were not following the example of Jesus, who was always spending intentional time with people who were different than he was.

Perhaps we as Christians can learn from the contributions of this social theory—and even more so, learn from the example of Jesus and help us truly understand how intentional and personal relationships can help us see the value of people for who they are, created in the image of God, deserving of respect and love. *Contact* can be more than just a method in how we approach others, but a way of life that follows the way Jesus lived in contact with others. After all, Jesus did come to extend his love to a broken humanity—one which, on one hand, he was nothing like in his divinity; but on the other, deeply related to in his humanity.

Practicing contact in our lives, as an active way of life, provides a highly needed benefit to our perspectives and understandings. Although Jesus represented the ultimate example of what it meant to come in contact with and engage and embrace others, he didn't come in contact with people *despite* who they were, what they looked like, or where they were from. He came in contact with people because his love *transcended* who they were, what they looked like, or where they came from.

Jesus didn't need to gain any perspectives in his journey, because he *was* the perspective. Understanding him meant understanding others. However, since we are not Jesus, and our thoughts and actions are always imperfect and incomplete compared to his, we have much to gain from striving to understand others and gaining their perspectives, built on the foundation of understanding the life and example of Jesus. First, we come in contact with others because Jesus has come in contact with us. Because Jesus' love transcends anything about who we are, what we look like, what our past is, or where we grew up, he still comes into unconditional contact with us. Therefore, we are spiritually and morally bound to come into unconditional contact with others, and our love should likewise transcend any barriers of who they are, what they look like, whatever their past may be, or where they grew up.

Contact can lead us to conciliation with groups we have normally generalized or dismissed in the past. But ultimately, until we come into contact with Jesus and are reconciled to God through him, all else in life falls short. Our greatest understanding is not found in human relationships, but in a divine relationship. And our perspectives, no matter how carefully composed or balanced, don't matter unless they are sought out of God's perspective.

Defining "Different" and Other Words

Going forward, I will use phrases and terms such as *people who are different, those from different backgrounds, those different from ourselves, outgroup members, the "other,"* etc. My appeal is to people whose lives may be conducive to a singular view of life and perspective. When we think about those who are different from ourselves while reading through this book, let's consider a variety of people. Consider people who may have grown up on the other side of town from you; those with a different skin color, socioeconomic status, immigration status, educational attainment, political affiliation, sexual orientation, age, religion, ability or disability, etc. In short, consider people who have a different life experience than you do.

We are surrounded by people different from us, in so many ways. We all represent unique persons created by God. Likewise, let's understand that there is so much value in understanding and learning about others who are different. When we are intentional about this—when we come into contact with people who represent a different experience from our own—we gain a more complete understanding not only of people, but of God.

I am also careful about using the word *prejudice,* as it might induce a sense of accusation and antagonism because the word has been categorized in such a way, but to be clear, simple definitions of prejudice are "preconceived judgment or opinion" and "an adverse opinion or leaning formed without just grounds or before sufficient knowledge."[2] Prejudice is a trait in all of us. At some point, we have all attributed preconceived opinions or shown unjust behaviors toward others that were not rooted in anything other than our emotions or our fear. Please understand that the intention of this book is not to make accusations, but rather to help people see a bigger picture of the incredible power of contact with others through the example of Jesus.

Mapping Our Path

Too often, we as human beings are quick to speak and slow to listen. We are quick to judge instead of help. We are quick to comment publicly, but slow to "private message" for the sake of trying to understand. We forget the value of intentional relationships with those who are different, because it's easy to live life in a bubble filled with one kind of people, one kind of news, one kind of church, or one kind of perspective. Through contact with others, walls are broken down and lines are crossed in positive ways.

Going forward, we will examine the theory behind contact, catch it up to what the Bible already says through biblical and theological examples, examine stories of people and initiatives that are successfully living out contact in their lives, discuss practical ways we can engage others, and understand the opportunities that we have in doing so.

My attempt in this book is to bring light, not heat—light of an understanding of contact in a way that we can adapt it to our relationships in our culture today. There is a better way forward than the current state of human relations and discourse. If we genuinely seek out relationships with those normally outside our world of thought and those who have different perspectives, we may not always come to agreement, but we can attain a level of respect and dignity about each other that is worth more than quickly categorizing someone based on their political views, skin color, worship style, cultural norms, etc. Ultimately, we will be able to see each other as made in the image of God, deserving our love, and recognize their worth, just as God recognizes all of our worth and extends his love to each one of us.

This book is primarily geared toward a US context and is written in that perspective; however, the contents and ideas presented in this book can be viewed as transcultural because the foundation and framework of this book—contact and relationship with Jesus—is transcultural.

This book is also written within the context of Christianity. However, my hope is that the main theme of this book—that intentional relationships develop perspective—can also provide valuable insight for those who may not adhere to a Christian worldview. My prayer is that those who read this work and do not have a transformative relationship with Jesus will see the value of a life and relationship with him—because these ideas started with him.

Humans always have and always will have division among each other in some form or another, because we live in an imperfect world. But when you enter into a life-filled relationship with Jesus, there is no division between you and God. Submitting to God and surrendering your life to him doesn't make any sense to many people; but when you come into contact with Jesus, know him, and form an intentional relationship with him, submitting to God and following him becomes the *only* thing that makes sense.

What This Book Is and What It's Not

This book is not about any problems the US may have today. It's about the value, respect, and dignity that all people deserve. It is about the value of intentional relationships with others and how personal encounters with those who are different from ourselves can bring about an understanding that leads to those relationships developing perspective and impacting our view of people and our view of who God is. Relationships may not always lead to agreement, but what they will do is produce a perspective of the other person and their experience that offers a bigger picture of who they are in the image of God.

I know I don't have all the answers or know everything there is to know about understanding others or understanding culture, and I want to always have a posture of learning and correction. But I am certain of something: I want to love people like Jesus did, and I want to urge others to do the same. This book is not about a lot of things, but it is about loving God and loving others, and living it out through actions and words.

CHAPTER 1

JOURNEYS

God designs journeys for every one of us. Not everyone has that "aha" moment or hears that divine voice coming from above (although some may), but everyone does have a journey that is intricately and uniquely designed by God. This chapter probably isn't the heaviest chapter in this book, but it's important because the story of how God has shaped my journey so far is probably similar to many others—especially in the sense that God uses events and conversations here and there, even if we don't realize them at the time, to shape who we are today.

God's journey for me led me to Georgia in late 2016, where I found myself thrust into a new life and a new culture like I had never experienced before. I began working in the area of Clarkston, GA, which is part of the metro Atlanta area and the epicenter for refugee resettlement in Georgia. It has been referred to as "the most diverse square mile in America" and the "Ellis Island of the South" because of its unique amalgam of people from all over the world.[3]

I was working as a case manager helping resettle refugees with World Relief, a nonprofit organization in the area. This gave me the privileged experience of many exciting yet challenging elements of the job, including picking refugees up at the airport, helping set up their housing, teaching them how to navigate grocery stores in the US, teaching them how to pay bills in the US, helping them learn how to budget their finances, enrolling them in ESL classes, enrolling children in school, helping them navigate the US healthcare system (do any of us really know how to do this?), and the list goes on.

My work with refugees impacted my worldview in substantial ways, and my move to Georgia contributed to the growth and nurturing of the way I loved others. It was my interactions and relationships with the "other" that helped develop my overall perspective of people, all made in God's image.

However, as much as my journey thrived from the relationships I developed in Georgia, it is not where my journey began. God ordained events in my life—some of which I learned from retroactively—that shaped who I am today and gave me the curiosity for culture that I have today.

I was born and raised in the midsized town of Columbus, Mississippi. I'm deeply and overall positively shaped by my upbringing in Mississippi. I am blessed to have the most caring and understanding parents anyone could ever ask to have. I was also blessed enough to have a very privileged upbringing—not as privileged as some, but certainly more privileged than most.

My cultural awareness growing up was existent, but very limited in depth. I had plenty of casual relationships and encounters with people from different cultural backgrounds, mostly African American, but I can't remember many that were very intentional. The racial demographics of Mississippi are approximately 59% Caucasian, 37% African American, and 3% Hispanic.[4] I didn't realize it at the time, but I was deeply surrounded by cultural differences, from which I could have learned much.

When I was in middle school and high school, I played basketball and interacted with my black teammates on a daily basis. We spent hours together at practices and games, in class, etc. Although I was spending a lot of time with them because they were my teammates and classmates, that was basically all they were. I didn't have any particular animosity toward them, and I would have never considered myself prejudiced or racist. I enjoyed the time I spent with them, and I would even have considered myself good friends with them back then; but nonetheless, I didn't fully understand how different some of their lives were from mine or how their expectations were set to a different standard than mine. I didn't really *know* or *understand* them—I didn't really strive for *contact* with them.

Looking back, we basically only spent time together during practices, games, or school. We didn't hang out on the weekends and go eat or go to the movies like I did with my white friends. I avoided conversations about differences such as politics, neighborhoods, family dynamics, etc., because I unconsciously knew those were differences I wasn't ready to understand or acknowledge. I knew these teammates and classmates of mine on a casual level, but I didn't know them on a personal and intentional level. Because of this, in my mind, it was easy to classify them as "them." It was easy to be separated from the understanding of who they were, what their families were like, what kind of neighborhoods they lived in, and their life experiences. If I knew what I know now at twenty-seven, I would have been much more intentional with those relationships.

As far as intentional and genuine relationships were concerned, my life was fairly singular in this aspect through high school and much of college. And because this aspect of my life was singular in many ways, so was my perspective and understanding. It wasn't until some of my experiences during and after college that I began to become more culturally aware and culturally curious.

As a member of the dominant cultural and social group (white male), it's not easy to intentionally expand from those dominant culture and social circles. I learned along the way that people only act off the information and lifestyle with which they surround themselves. If we only surround ourselves with similar people and similar ideas, it's natural that we will produce a singular worldview and an understanding of the world and other people in comparison to our own cultural background. But when we open ourselves up to a plurality of people, our understanding of people expands and our worldview gains more depth.

That is the main focus and challenge of this book: to intentionally expand ourselves from our own cultural understandings through personal relationships with people different from ourselves and from different cultural backgrounds. The substance of this writing is birthed in the idea that intentional relationships affect our perspectives, and this is my appeal because our diversity in relationships also impacts our ability and desire to love. Through this, we realize the *Imago Dei* in people more completely, and realize the love and capability of God more fully.

A Stranger in Mexico

In the spring of 2015, I spent several weeks in Mexico working with some local churches. One afternoon, I traveled with a minister of one of the churches I was with at the time to a rural area where another member of the church lived. The visit, of course, included a delicious meal of some traditional Mexican dishes. I enjoyed my time visiting and fellowshipping with the families that were in attendance.

Shortly after our meal, many of us were standing outside continuing to talk, and one of the women came out of the house with an empty pitcher in her hand. I don't remember the exact order of the events that ensued, because I wasn't paying close attention at the time, but I remember her walking with the pitcher away from the house. She returned just a few minutes later with the pitcher filled with a yellow-green colored liquid. I was given an empty glass, confused as to what this liquid was for a moment, until it dawned on me that it was cactus juice she had just freshly retrieved from a cactus out in the field. She poured me a glass, and I could feel the warm temperature of the cactus juice radiating through the glass into my hand. I took a quick smell and was not pleased at all by the aroma.

I have to admit sometimes it was fun being the only American person in groups like this because you received more attention than normal, and this time was no different. All eyes were on me as I was being offered this glass of cactus juice, which didn't look good or smell good. I'm usually really open to trying new foods and drinks, but with this I hesitated. I continued to look at it and smell it, and as I continued to hesitate I heard comments like, "It's good for your heart," and "It's good, try it!" So I took a sip, and my intuition was correct; my taste buds were not satisfied. Everyone got a laugh out of the American trying fresh cactus juice for the first time, and it ended up being a comical story to tell.

Stories like this and other international experiences of getting to know people and their culture helped catalyze my curiosity for culture. Looking back now, my short time in Mexico was perhaps the genesis of later seasons in life that were pivotal in the shaping of the way I thought about the world and about people, even though I didn't realize it at the time.

My tasks in Mexico were to preach and teach and to assist the ministers of the churches with any other tasks as necessary. The congregations there didn't necessarily need to hear from a young American, but overall it was a blessing to give the usual ministers a break. Each church was located in a different city, so I stayed in each location for about two weeks. At the time, my Spanish was not very good (I'm still practicing today), especially to preach or teach. So instead of risking mixing up the word "sin" (*pecado*) with the word "fish" (*pescado*) and telling people that fish separated them from God, I was blessed enough to have access to an interpreter in each location.

There was one interpreter in particular who continued to probe me about US immigration laws while offering up his own personal story of migration to the US. Paraphrasing from my memory, he told me he traveled along the Rio Grande for several days to get to the US, and when he was there all he wanted to do was an honest job. I was very quick to disregard him at the time, even when he told me to look up some Bible verses about the topic, because immigration was not a subject I was very familiar with. I responded to him not with much challenge or negativity; nonetheless, I was very slow to truly listen to his story and hear his perspective. In my mind I was quick to judge him only by the law. That may have been appropriate in some ways, but instead of making quick judgments and dismissing him, I should have listened better, whether I agreed with him at the time or not.

Thankfully, he was not the only person I had conversations with about immigration. Being in Mexico, I met several people who had immigrated to the US; whether legally or unauthorized, they all had a personal story. A member of a different church whom I was able to get to know, Sergio, was a seasonal farm worker in Texas with documented status. He worked seasonally, managing a watermelon farm. Sergio would travel to Texas several weeks out of the year to help harvest watermelons. This was the primary way he earned income for his family. Most people would agree that the economy and living conditions in Mexico are not equal to that of the US. Yes, there are some wealthy regions in the country; however, the gap between the rich and poor is much greater and money does not go quite as far. The economic burden that plagues many Mexican families is one of the driving forces of Mexican immigration.

Although my intentions in Mexico were good and my time there was fruitful, God was shaping who I am today through small conversations along the way back then. From my perspective, I was a stranger in Mexico. In many of the places I visited, I was the only person around who looked like me (a redheaded, pale white guy)—a circumstance that I rarely, if ever, had found myself in before. But in my journey, I have learned that sometimes it takes being a stranger to understand a stranger.

Contemplative Travels

The summer of 2018 brought me on a short volunteer opportunity with refugee ministries in Austria and Greece. At a men's camp I was helping out at in Greece, during one worship night, someone had mentioned that there were eleven different nationalities represented at the camp. Singing songs and hearing the voices of men of so many different nationalities from around the world puts you in a special place. It was a place I had never been before, and the one thing I was focused on at the time was how this moment was a glimpse of heaven, and that we have an incredible eternity to look forward to.

I was familiar with being surrounded by different cultures on a regular basis through my work with World Relief, but this part of my journey and this specific worship night offered a different perspective than I had gained previously. Many of the refugees I encountered here had just made the journey to Athens, several of them from Afghanistan and Iran. Many had left their homes because of their newfound faith in Christ. Others were seekers who had fled their home countries for other reasons, but were trying to find new life in Athens or further into Europe, where some had family members who went ahead of them.

The contemplation I witnessed with many of these people was striking. Many of them were contemplating what it meant to follow Jesus and if it was worth giving up friends and family. Others contemplated their next decisions on the next place to go, or even if the governments would allow them to go. And others contemplated staying in Greece and building their new lives there.

I had heard plenty of stories about the travels of refugees and the difficult decisions they faced, but in Austria and Greece I was able to witness their contemplation in action. I learned that with many of them, contemplation was a part of their journey—but frequently, ineluctability outweighed contemplation, and they were forced to make the decision to leave the life they had known forever.

It was here that I contemplated and strengthened my own under-standing of what it meant to leave everything and follow Jesus. Not only that, but I observed that the faith of many of the new believers I encountered was often stronger than that of many, if not most, Americans I knew. The reason I narrowed it down to was their sense of contemplation.

For myself, and for many others who grow up in the US, we don't have much at all to consider—or much, if anything, to give up—when making the decision to follow Jesus. For us, consider-ing abandoning our homeland or our families to follow Jesus, or for other reasons of persecution, seems foreign. It's hard to realize and understand until we are able to spend time with people who come from those backgrounds and have had those experiences.

I understand that not everyone has the geographical or logisti-cal opportunities it might take to witness culture and perspective in this specific way. However, most of us are surrounded by diverse cultures in our own cities, whether we realize it or not. It's not just migrants who offer us cultural perspective, but any demographic or social group of which you are not a part.

I am blessed to have been able to form relationships with close friends who are African American, Asian, Middle Eastern, and more. We are friends because we have many things in common and similar interests. But even more deeply, we are able to also bond over what makes us different, including the ways we grew up and the cultural backgrounds we came from. My journey still has a long way to go, and I still have much to learn, but I'm encouraged by the relation-ships I have made with people who are not like me, and thankful for the impact it has had on my perspective, which has ultimately impacted my ability to love others well and see the *Imago Dei* in everyone. Here's to everyone out there on this journey. May our love for others and our love for God be the drive of that journey.

Discussion

1. Observe the journey you have been on so far. Looking back, what
   are some events or conversations God has used to shape you, even
   if you didn't realize it at the time?

2. How did your upbringing and environment shape who you are
   today and your understanding of people? Discuss specifics such as
   your family, friendships, and relationships at school or on teams.

3. Have you ever been a stranger in any place? How were you able
   to adapt to the people and environment? (Majority and minority
   culture people may perceive this question differently.)

4. How did being a stranger help you better understand what some people feel on a regular basis?

5. What places have you traveled domestically or internationally that have helped shape who you are today, through the relationships you built there?

6. When you became a Christian, do you remember contemplating that decision?

7. Have you been through a season of life, even after you chose to follow Jesus, where you contemplated that decision or asked a lot of questions that resulted in a strengthened faith?

8. How can we better empathize with people like refugees, who seriously contemplate the life-altering decision to follow Jesus?

9. How can we shape our journeys going forward in ways that will help us better understand people different from us?

CHAPTER 2

CONTACT

Remembering the Titans

In 1954, the US Supreme Court case Brown v. Board of Education became a landmark decision in declaring racial segregation in public schools unconstitutional. This decision effectively overturned the 1896 Supreme Court case Plessy v. Ferguson, which had formed the "separate, but equal" doctrine.[5] Although the Brown ruling marked a pivotal moment and served as a catalyst in the path toward school integration and civil rights, its implementation would face a variety of social opposition. Because the ruling didn't specify exactly how to end school segregation, combined with resistance at the local levels, the goal of desegregation still had a long way to go. It took several other local and federal court rulings along the way to clarify the implementation and enforce desegregation. However, it was ultimately because of the legal precedent of Brown v. Board of Education, and several other laws and landmark bills like the Civil Rights Act, that integration was able to occur. This point will prove important as we dive deeper into understanding the principle of contact.

Hostility at the local level was one of the largest hurdles for desegregation to overcome. Several events around the country, especially in Southern states, took place that prolonged the integration of schools for several years after the initial Brown ruling: The Southern Manifesto, Governor George Wallace notoriously blocking the door to Foster Auditorium at the University of Alabama, and James Meredith's trials enrolling into the University of Mississippi.

There were also more subtle events and local themes that contributed to the maintenance of segregated schools despite the Supreme Court's ruling. Neighborhood housing patterns caused continued segregation, which in turn caused continued segregation of local schools.[6] Through the Swann v. Charlotte-Mecklenburg ruling in 1971, courts approved busing and other methods to remedy the role that residential segregation had in the path toward school integration.[7]

Effects of events like these were chronicled in such movies like *Remember the Titans*, the 2000 dramatization film that depicted the T. C. Williams High School 1971 football team and the surrounding events in Alexandria, VA. Although the film uses some creative license to dramatize the events at the time, it is still based on true events, and the film also serves as a great example of what successful contact can look like.

It's the summer of 1971, and the football players who had previously attended an all-white school were now learning that they would be sharing T. C. Williams High School with black students in an effort to desegregate the high schools in the city. The school board had selected Herman Boone, a black man, to be head coach of the football team over Bill Yoast, a white man, who had more experience. Yoast at first rejected the offer of assistant coach, but after learning that many of the white players he had previously coached at a different school the year before were threatening to quit, Yoast decided to accept the offer, not wanting to see any of his players miss scholarship opportunities.

Upon his decision, Yoast leads his players into the gymnasium where the black players and Coach Boone are gathered, initially thinking they would not have an integrated football team. The black players and white players lock in on each other, and the journey to a long football season began.

A majority of the film chronicles the team's challenges in training camp at Gettysburg College. As the teams board the buses to go to training camp, Coach Boone notices that they are boarding in a segregated fashion. He decides to organize the buses by offense and defense, effectively mixing blacks and whites, and further tells them that the persons they are sitting next to will be their roommates at training camp. At training camp, the black and white players are forced to live together, practice together, eat in the same vicinity, and spend the majority of their time together. As a result, many racially induced altercations and arguments occur.

As the team begins to spend more time together, and with inspiration from the coaching staff, the players begin to respect each other, and some even become close friends. There is the iconic scene where the team is practicing late at night and Gerry's friend Ray (both are white) gives a lackadaisical effort on offense and is then confronted by Gerry for not blocking, while Julius (black) and the other players look on. On the following play, Julius sticks the quarterback and it fires up Gerry, who compliments Julius: "You really stuck him, Campbell!" To which Julius appropriately replies, "Yeah, I love me a little contact!" (See what I did there?) Gerry then playfully shoves Julius with his arm and yells, "Left side!" And after a few seconds Julius affirms Gerry's gesture by returning the shove, yelling, "Strong side!" And both players go back and forth a few times while the players and coaches watch in awe, as this is seemingly the first time a black and white player have mutually got along, setting the tone for the rest of the movie. I get chills every time I watch this scene.

The common goal of winning seems to be what initially unites the Titans and fosters group cooperation. This film highlights what it means to come in contact with people who are different, and how contact can form positive intergroup relations. For the Titans, their initial racial animosity toward each other was strong because they didn't know each other. They only knew that the "other" was a different color, came from a different background, and represented what seemed to be different values. However, as chronicled in the film, their face-to-face contact, combined with other elements that will be examined later, resulted in decreased prejudice toward each other. They were able to embrace each other's differences and work toward the common goal of winning.

Can we learn any lessons about intergroup relations from *Remember the Titans*? What if we proactively approached our relationships with those different from us through intentional contact with them? This chapter will examine what contact is and how its effects can have positive impacts on the way we build relationships and view people different from ourselves.

What Is Contact?

What happens when people interact? This depends on how you interpret "interact." Some of my convictions and motivations for writing this book are based upon encounters I've had in my own life with people from different cultures, but they also stem from stories I've heard from others about how their relationships with people from different cultures have impacted and developed their cultural competence. I've heard stories about how developing intentional relationships with coworkers and classmates has increased tolerance and empathy while decreasing generalizations or other negative attributes associated with the specific group as a whole. To put it simply, relationship-based intentional contact with others who are different from us and/or represent different worldviews provide us with a path toward positive interaction with them, resulting in a deeper respect and deeper ability to love others well.

This book is about the incredible power of contact, not only in the form of relational contact with others, but also in understanding how God has made contact with us through Jesus, as a way to be reconciled to him, and because of this supernatural and sacrificial contact of love, we are obliged to seek loving contact with others different from ourselves. Jesus has not held our differentness and otherness against us; our contact with him is unconditional. Therefore, we make no conditions in our contact with others.

A good definition of "contact" is (1) *relationship-based intentional bonding and/or communication with members of different cultural or social groups who share differing backgrounds and perspectives unfamiliar to one's own;* or (2) *relationship-based intentional bonding and/or communication with anyone who holds different or unfamiliar perspectives or worldviews.* The first definition is the essence of this book. The second definition is meant to serve as evidence that contact, when properly carried out, is transrelational, meaning that contact can be successful in almost any situation, taking almost any difference into account.

Contact is similar to the idea of proximity and being in the presence of others. Proximity is a powerful tool that helps us get to where we need to be to understand others. Contact is proximity and more. It's learning who people are, where they come from, how they grew up, what has impacted their lives, trials they have faced that you haven't, how they view the world and why they view it that way, and more. Everyone has been influenced or learned the perspectives they hold in a unique way that is always different from one person to the next. Just because they may subscribe to a different line of thought on a subject or even a completely different worldview doesn't necessarily mean that it's wrong; if you had grown up in the same context as that person, you might well hold to the same lines of thinking.

This is true of groups and larger cultures as well. Different cultural groups share different ways and views of life. A simple example of this is when an American travels to a country like Germany and encounters the stereotype of German people being rude. It is not until the American spends some time in the culture and gets to closely know some of the German people that he or she realizes that the rudeness they thought they encountered early on is a cultural difference rooted in a direct and explicit communication style. Germans being "rude," as an American might interpret it, is actually just them being very straightforward and a sign of respect because they do not want to sugarcoat anything. This principle of cultural understanding, developed after gaining more contact with a culture, can also be applied in our everyday relationships.

Contact can be the most effective way to decrease prejudice and increase understanding. Not only can contact increase our understandings of different cultural values, but we can also learn to appreciate the different points of views that people from different cultures hold. When we intentionally get to know and learn about each other, we begin to see that perspectives and worldviews are not just arbitrary views used for personal or political gain, but deeply rooted histories that tell a larger story of the culture and its experiences as a whole.

Why Do We Need Contact?

Intentional contact can be the basis by which many of our broken relationships in society can be mended. Just as we encounter and have contact with Jesus to mend our brokenness, contact with our neighbors can have the same effect. We need contact because it serves an intentional purpose in the way we interact with and treat others. We need contact because the world is growing; we are encountering more diversity than ever before. We need a way to help increase our cultural competence so we will be able to better communicate, understand, and respect those of different cultures, or even those within our own cultures with whom we have difficulty.

We also need contact to address the growing polarization in our political systems. Developing perspective in this area can be seen as extremely divisive, but it also helps us understand so many other subjects of great importance in our society. When we address those with different perspectives on topics like the criminal justice system, healthcare, immigration, and other issues under the social justice umbrella Christians should care about, we are responding to the larger political economy that has become so separated. By doing so, perhaps, we can dwindle the binary posture of our ideological systems.

Our social media ecosystem also plays into this growing polarization, divisive rhetoric, and prejudice. Fake news, comment sections, pundit websites, and more all feed into information bubbles that many people live in, as they hear only one perspective about a subject that will continually lead them into antagonism toward other competing perspectives. This is an extremely unhealthy way to take in news and information. We as Christians must learn how to better filter our information and better hear the perspectives of others, even our non-Christian neighbors. We can't operate under the assumption that views outside of our usual communities of thought are inherently wrong.

I can't tell you how many times I've read an article on a network news outlet that has no political nature to it, and yet the comment sections are filled with dehumanizing and hateful rhetoric about a political party or person. Social media, in many ways, has become a sounding board for people who live in an information bubble, who want the world to hear what they have to say yet will not do the work it takes to present a balanced or respectful comment.

Disagreements will always exist. The goal of contact is not a perfect alignment of perspectives or values; rather, it is meant for each party to better understand the perspectives and values the other holds. In this way, we are more equipped to love one another and not diminish what makes us different. We are able to see each other as uniquely created in the image of God, deserving of respect and dignity and love. Love beautifully binds together our differences and creates a display that is threaded together by all of us.

What Does Contact Look Like?

So what does contact look like on a practical level? In a later chapter, we will examine some practical ways to implement this intentional approach to others as well as examine some successful contact stories. In general, though, contact can be accomplished by and through many relationships that already exist in our life—eating lunch with a coworker who you know holds different political views, getting a small group at your church to sponsor and help a recently arrived refugee family, or spending time with someone thirty years older or thirty years younger. Opportunities are all around us.

One of the greatest ways we can learn is by saying, "I'm trying to understand this better; what are your thoughts on this?" We desperately need the ability to exit our information bubbles and take in multiple perspectives, so we can better discern and develop our thoughts on a particular subject. We will build on what contact looks like as we go along, but for now, I want to note that we don't pursue contact with others just to expand our diversity portfolio. We should pursue contact with others in order to learn how to love them better.

Contact in History

To gain a better understanding of how we got here, it is essential to briefly examine contact theory in history. There is a fairly large field of scholarship focused on contact theory and its effects. Christians have yet to put such focus on how contact can lead to growth of perspective and general conciliation. And yet, the research that exists and largely supports contact theory as a means to reduce prejudice and increase understanding just needs to be caught up to what the Bible already teaches and what God already desires. My hope is that the ideas brought forth in this book will serve as a springboard for churches, organizations, and individuals to utilize contact as a serious way to engage with others.

Contact theory emerged in the discipline of social psychology in the 1930s and 1940s as a result of the "field's focus on intergroup relations and interaction between people within a social context."[8] Several decades ago, before Gordon Allport released his groundbreaking work *The Nature of Prejudice,* researchers began examining the effects of intergroup contact as a means to reduce intergroup prejudice. Here is a brief, non-comprehensive timeline leading up to Allport's work:

> 1945: Interracial experiences could lead to "mutual understanding and regard."[9]

> 1946: When groups "are isolated from one another, prejudice and conflict grow like a disease."[10]

> 1946: "After the desegregation of the Merchant Marine, genuine bonds developed between black and white seamen on the ships and in the maritime union."[11]

> 1946: "Prejudiced attitudes toward minorities of White students at Dartmouth College and Harvard University diminished directly to the extent that they had had equal-status contact with the minorities."[12]

> 1947: "Intergroup contact would maximally reduce prejudice when the two groups share similar status, interests, and tasks and when the situation fosters personal, intimate intergroup contact."[13]

1951: "White women in the desegregated projects had far more optimal contact with their black neighbors. Moreover, they held their black neighbors in higher esteem and expressed greater support for interracial housing"[14]

Other studies around this time indicated the positive effects of interracial housing on intergroup attitudes. Keep in mind that these studies reported positive results before most important civil rights legislation was passed.

Building off recent interracial housing studies at the time, Allport introduced the most influential study of intergroup contact to date, *The Nature of Prejudice* (1954), which continues to be a foundational force for continuing and expanding research in the field. Numerous reviews since Allport have evidenced general support for contact theory, suggesting that intergroup contact typically reduces intergroup prejudice. However, there is a need to acknowledge that, as with most other social psychological theories, there have been some reviews that have produced more mixed and critical results, which Pettigrew describes as having incomplete samples of relevant papers, their absence of strict inclusion rules, and nonquantitative assessments of contact effects.[15]

On What Conditions?

According to Allport's research, merely putting different people in the same room or different social groups in the same neighborhood does not always result in healthy contact or increased understanding; in fact, there are several examples of contact that never really produced increased perspective (more on this later). For example, we may work with or go to school with others from a different social group, but this does not always result in healthy relationships and mutual understandings of the persons or their social groups as a whole. Allport recognized this in his research, and posited four positive conditions required for contact to be successful:

1. Equal status between groups
2. Common goals
3. Intergroup cooperation
4. Support from authorities

When we take into account what factors need to be in place for contact to be successful, these conditions are guiding principles that can help us. There has been scholarship produced since Allport that suggests these conditions are not always necessary, and that just being in the presence of outgroup members can reduce prejudice and increase understanding. Nonetheless, these conditions are important to take into account when we think about genuine contact as a whole.

Equal Status

Equal status can be interpreted in a variety of ways, depending on which perspective you're looking at it from. Much of the time, outgroup members will be of a different status—socioeconomic, immigration, political, education, and so on. So when we approach contact situations and consider if all parties have equal standing, we should consider equal status *within* the situation.[16]

For Christians, this can mean challenging ourselves to not use our status to our advantage, but rather to humble ourselves and take the form of a servant, just as Jesus did and calls us to do (Phil. 2:5–7). Especially for majority-culture people, we must consider how our status impacts others and how we can continue to work toward equal status for others. Just as in *Remember the Titans*, we won't pretend like the black players' experiences mean equal status, but on the football field within the limits of the team, they did. Every player had an equal opportunity to prove himself.

Common Goals

Increasing our understanding and reducing our negative generalizations toward others require common goals to be in place. This was evident in *Remember the Titans*; the players' animosity toward one another was remedied as they began working toward the common goal of winning a state championship. Interracial athletic teams represent a great example of working toward a common goal and overcoming prejudice.[17]

The obvious commonality that Christians share and continue to work toward is our faith in Jesus. We often hear people say how we should put our differences aside and unite around Jesus. Of course we should unite and look toward Jesus as the one who unites us all, but we should not overlook how we can also learn from the different features within Christianity.

Christianity presents itself differently in different cultures, in the US and all over the world. The systems of the Western church look dramatically different than those of churches in Africa or East Asia. Sure, there may be some elements in some settings that are questionable; but overall, they are all beautiful expressions of the nations uniquely worshipping Jesus.

But not everyone is a Christian. So when contact is necessary with people who do not have the same faith as us, we have to think about what unites us as a collective world, what is good for us, and what we need. As Christians, we will never be able to separate ourselves from what makes us who we are, and the non-Christian must also respect the differences at stake as well. But when it comes to common goals, surely we can always find something within the situation that will help bring us together and help us to better understand each other.

Intergroup Cooperation

Intergroup cooperation requires noncompetitive striving toward a common goal.[18] When our emphasis is on competition instead of cooperation, we are less likely to view the other as an equal, and our generalizations are likely to maintain. We should also be careful to not engage in contact for the sole purpose of increasing the diversity of our social network and to show off our cultural competence for personal gain; this can lead to a competition-based element of our engagement with others and will not ultimately fulfill us. Instead, we should strive for genuine understanding and real relationships that are morphed out of cooperation, not competition.

I'm reminded of the relationship between the Jews and Gentiles in the New Testament when both groups had begun following the Way. There was some confusion about whether or not the Gentiles should partake in Jewish customs such as circumcision and further proselyte conversion. This can be viewed as an example of competition versus cooperation—not competition in the sense that Jews at that time were competing *against* Gentiles, but rather that they needed guidance on how to navigate the competing beliefs they had known their whole lives.

These advocates, known as Judaizers, insisted that for Gentiles to follow Christ, they must convert to Judaism first. Paul describes how he addressed this to Peter: "[We] know that a person is not justified by the works of the law, but by faith in Jesus Christ. So we, too, have put our faith in Christ Jesus that we may be justified by faith in Christ and not by the works of the law, because by the works of the law no one will be justified" (Gal. 2:16). By this, Paul dismantled the notion and competing narrative that Gentiles should embrace all Jewish customs and values; rather, Gentiles were justified only by their faith. Likewise, the Jews did not need to forget or remove their Jewish marks or culture (1 Cor. 7:17–18). By maintaining both views, Paul revealed God's cosmic plan for the cooperation of his people and uniting them for worship under the one true God.

Support of Authorities

The last condition is concerned with support and the role of authorities in contact situations. Contact can be more efficient and effective with the support of authorities.[19] Alluding again to *Remember the Titans*, the players not only were under the auspices of the federal and local governments but also had a support structure from their coaches, who were their most direct authorities in the situation.

When it comes to intergroup contact, Christians can be comforted by the fact that we are supported by the ultimate Authority, who sanctions cultural and racial harmony and is continuing to restore his people through that.

However, support from authorities, as it can be vague and specific to circumstances, may not always be viewed the same by everyone. Like equal status, there are systems in place that impact how different people view what it actually means to be supported by authorities. If you're a majority-culture person, always be wary of only interpreting support through your lens; a minority may have a different experience with whoever the authority is in the situation.

How Do We Apply These Conditions in Our Contexts?

There are instances when the conditions described above cannot be met, and sometimes may not be required at all. For example, attaining equal status between all parties involved may not be possible. However, we must continue to remind ourselves of the way Jesus, despite his superior status, chose to "humble himself, being made like a servant." There are situations where we are called to do the same. When we think about conciliation, or how best to understand someone's position, it sometimes seems almost impossible because there is no way we can relate; our circumstances are so different. But when we try to emulate Jesus, humble ourselves, and take on the heart of a servant, we begin to serve and begin to listen.

In situations where contact is needed, we can ask ourselves questions such as:

- How can I humble myself and show empathy without making my status, whether greater or lesser, a focal point of our relationship or conversation?

- What are some common goals we have that we can utilize as a path toward understanding?

- How can we work toward those goals while recognizing and being respectful of our differences?

- In what ways am I cooperating in this relationship as we understand or work toward our common goals? In what ways am I not cooperating, and being competitive instead?

- What support can we recognize from authorities?

Considering these questions in relationships or conversations with others different from ourselves, we are able to more effectively and efficiently understand each other. We must always keep in mind that conditions aren't our authority—our authority is God, and he has created everyone uniquely in his image.

A Few Notes to Consider on these Conditions

Although these conditions are important and should be considered in contact moments, it may be better if they are interpreted as a way to better *facilitate* successful contact. Recent research suggests that not all of these conditions are required at the same time in every contact situation.[20]

So yes, let's consider some of these conditions as we approach relationships with others and consider them through the lens of Jesus and how he approached relationships with others. But let's not let these conditions hold us back from contact opportunities just because one or more are not there or are not easily implementable. Let's strive to do what we can to continually move in this direction.

Casual Encounter vs. Genuine Relationship

Contact is only as successful as the person who is motivated to utilize it. We must actively live out contact in our everyday lives, and this means seeking genuine relationships over casual encounters. The difference between casual encounters and genuine, intentional relationships with outgroup members is substantial.

When we consider what it means to have genuine contact with someone different, what does that mean and how does that work? We have casual encounters every day with outgroup members at our jobs, schools, public places, and more, but these relationships often do not progress to friendship. Friendship is a key factor in considering what it means to have genuine contact. Much of the time, for contact to have positive effects, there must be a real friendship that is produced or continually worked toward. In friendships, many of the conditions previously listed are already in place, or more easily implemented, such as common goals, cooperation, and equal status.[21] Evidence shows us that intergroup interactions through cross-cultural friendships promotes positive effects of contact.[22] Pettigrew also cites research conducted in Northern Ireland that examined cross-group friendships among Catholics and Protestants, which resulted in forgiveness and trust during times of sectarian violence.[23] We will discuss more on friendships later.

In a similar fashion, when we think about our relationship with God, is it a daily casual encounter, or is it an intimate and growing relationship where we continue to learn and understand him more each day? Our understanding and perspective of others can only grow by spending time with them and getting to know them. Intimacy plays a role in our understanding of others as well as our understanding of God. Are we passively accepting our daily encounters with others, or are we actively pursuing relationships with people who can teach us and grow our perspective, not just them for them but as who God created them to be? Are we passively accepting God in our lives or actively pursuing him? As we continue to strive to love God in all things, let us also continue to love others in all situations.

Going Forward

As we move along, challenge yourself to think about relationships with people different from yourself in your life right now, whether daily casual encounters or already well-established relationships, and about the ways in which you perceive them as individuals and as part of their group as a whole. Think about what has influenced you to think about them that way, whether positively or negatively. Think about the differences you have with them and how those differences influence your perception of them, and ask yourself why these differences exist at all. Try to understand how your feelings toward what is different about them can help you understand them as individuals better, as well as help you understand the group they are a part of better. Think about the commonalities you share, and how similar interests and goals can be used as a springboard to a more complete mutual understanding.

Discussion

1. What is your understanding of contact so far?

2. Are you typically more hesitant or more willing to engage people who are different from you? Why?

3. Do you consciously or unconsciously set conditions for getting to know certain types or groups of people? Why do you think you do this?

4. Do you currently have any casual relationships in your life that have the potential to be genuine? What could you possibly learn through these relationships if they were more intentional?

5. Do you have any current relationships with people different from you that were the result of positive contact?

CHAPTER 3

COMMUNICATION, INFORMATION, AND CONTACT

The current state of communication between people and how people receive information, including many Christians, is in need of some purification. Lawless social media comment sections, subscription to incredulous news authorities, submission to political parties and figures, unfiltered pundit and opinion websites, and more are contributing to the growing polarization between many people. This induces a hesitation, or even a complete lack of attempting, to truly understand differing perspectives that aren't already a part of one's current information world. The division is real and it's growing. Anecdotally, we see it and hear it. Statistically, the data proves it.

Pew Research has been tracking political polarization across ten dimensions since 1994. One study, which surveyed more than five thousand adults, indicated that the average partisan gap has increased from 15 percentage points in 1994 to 36 points in 2017; this number has risen consistently across almost every data set collected since Pew began tracking this in 1994.[24] Unfavorability ratings have also seen dramatic increases. "Currently, 44% of Democrats and those who lean Democrat have a very unfavorable opinion of the GOP, based on yearly averages of Pew Research Center surveys; 45% of Republicans and those who lean Republican view the Democratic Party very unfavorably. In 1994, fewer than 20% in both parties viewed the opposing party very unfavorably."[25]

How did we get to this point, and how is the way people consume information related to how we develop perspectives and show respect for others who are different from us? What kind of responsibility do Christians have when it comes to filtering all the information and news thrown at us today? These are a few of the questions we will examine in this chapter.

The Search for Truth

A November 2016 headline of a *Washington Post* article read, "'Post-truth' Named 2016 Word of the Year by Oxford Dictionaries."[26] The accompanying article had a photo of Donald Trump and Hillary Clinton in what looked like a presidential debate atmosphere. The word, "post-truth," had seen an increase in usage during the 2016 presidential campaign. It was perhaps the most divisive campaign in modern history with name calling, attack ads, fake news, and *alternative facts* filling our media ecosystems.

I can't speak for all people, but I, and I assume many others, began to question what objective information actually was and how it was being supplied to the general public. For some, perhaps they began to question which sources to trust and which ones were misleading. For others, the way they filtered information was only strengthened toward a specific side.

For such a time in history when people are polarized enough to live in completely different dimensions of information and communication, how do we determine who and what is right? Is truth becoming more relative, or do we just need to reevaluate the way that we deliver, receive, and interpret information?

So, *do* we live in a post-truth age? Oxford Dictionaries defines post-truth as "relating to or denoting circumstances in which objective facts are less influential in shaping public opinion than appeals to emotion and personal belief."[27] It is possible for some people to be exposed to a certain type of misinformation, and without investigation of its validity, that misinformation can be constantly reinforced through their information world and, as some have called it, echo chambers. Without engaging in thorough research to determine how the information was gathered, truth can be exaggerated or, at worst, completely distorted.

There are also cases in which people are so engulfed in their information worlds that when misinformation is presented and then corrected, their beliefs in the initial misinformation are actually strengthened. This is likely, and partly due to singular news perspectives, as well as the threat that corrections will differ from one's worldview or the way they think things are supposed to be. Our current media ecosystems don't make it easy for anyone to filter balanced information, but as we continue in pursuit of truth, we must be open to corrections when they are presented; and when we receive new information, it should be calculated against our original information to form a balanced thought process of all the information.

The Backfire Effect

One example of this is a study conducted by political scientists, the results published in an article titled "When Corrections Fail: The Persistence of Political Misperceptions." One of the goals of the study was to see if misperceptions which can easily distort public opinion can be corrected. Participants were asked to read a mock news article about a campaign speech by President Bush in October 2004, then asked to read a correction of the article that included a report by the CIA documenting a lack of weapons of mass destruction (WMDs) in Iraq.

One of the lines, spoken by Bush, in the first version of the article read: "There was a risk, a real risk, that Saddam Hussein would pass weapons or materials or information to terrorist networks, and in the world after September the 11th, that was a risk we could not afford to take." Bush maintained that Iraq was a place where terrorists might get weapons of mass destruction. The wording of this sentence could have suggested that Saddam Hussein actually did have WMDs that he could have passed to other terrorist groups after September 11, 2001.

Half the participants were then given the corrected version, which included the CIA report that noted no evidence of WMDs in Iraq or an active production program immediately before the US invasion. They were then asked to measure their responses on the following statement: "Immediately before the US invasion, Iraq had an active weapons of mass destruction program, the ability to produce these weapons, and large stockpiles of WMDs, but Saddam Hussein was able to hide or destroy these weapons right before US forces arrived." For many participants, the corrected version did not change their beliefs about WMDs in Iraq; it actually *strengthened* it.[28]

The researchers in this study called this a *backfire effect*, because the expected result of being given factual information actually backfired and caused the participants, who already had predispositions, to actually strengthen their prior beliefs. If there is a strong motivation to hold on to a certain belief, then corrections are usually ineffective, as described by much of the scholarship on this topic. Some of these conclusions may be the result of ideology and source mismatches (the one used in this study was the Associated Press). However, regardless of perceived bias of the news source, we should try to carefully consider new developments and new perspectives.

WMDs aside, the backfire effect chronicled here is something that can be attributed to some of us. When something challenges our current way of thinking or something we are sure about, we tend to be resistant to new or correct information because we are afraid of being wrong or changing our minds because it might come off as a sign of weakness. In the current state of communication and information-gathering, we are drawn to spheres of influence that are sometimes right and sometimes wrong, but the more we continue to be drawn into those spheres, the more we begin to become blind to when those influences are wrong instead of right. Our ability to interpret and filter information becomes diminished when we are only exposed to one world of information that only continually confirms what we already believed, whether our predisposed beliefs are right or not to begin with. Often, it is not that we are *uninformed*, but rather that we are *misinformed*.

Media outlets, particularly in the US, have become servants of a select few audiences—and those audiences, servants of their chosen media outlets. However, when we take a hard look at where we are getting our information, we know that no media outlet is perfect and that, yes, some media outlets *probably* do distort, misrepresent, and exaggerate some of the information to serve their audiences or for other agendas. On the other hand, there are genuine and committed journalists who care about truth and relay that truth to any audience that is listening.

But in a world of confusion and distortion about information, how do we navigate it all?

Christians and Media Responsibility

We all have to do more work than we may want these days to understand information and truth. Even statistics require examining methodologies and multiple sources in order to gain a more complete perspective. As Christians, we have a responsibility to try to correctly navigate and filter information. After all, the religion of Christianity is the only religion that was created and is sustained by *news*—that is, the good news of the arrival, life, death, burial, resurrection, and eventual return of Jesus. [29] Without this news being true, Christianity would not be sustained. If Jesus was never actually resurrected from the grave, his disciples would have felt like they had wasted the last three years of their lives. The news of Jesus' resurrection sparked a movement that started with a few people and grew to billions today. The good news of Jesus is what continues to sustain Christianity today; we are driven by the truth that Jesus did what he said he came to do, and that as a result we are reconciled to God for eternity.

Our responsibility as Christians, therefore, is to try to correctly filter and interpret news. Because Christ is the greatest news of all, we are held to a standard of truth that should be different from the rest of the world. In addition, our responsibility to news is more important than ever because of the current news climate we live in. In the end, we will never agree on every topic, but we can set an example of good conduct on how to navigate our information-saturated world.

Filtering through All the Information

There is a principle of examination described in Acts 17 when Paul and Silas were in Berea. Verse 11b says, "they [the Bereans] received the message with great eagerness and examined the Scriptures every day to see if what Paul said was true." The Bereans exemplified incredible integrity. They were exposed to information they had read about in prophecies, but their first reaction was not to believe but to discern for themselves whether the information they were receiving was reliable. Interestingly, the following verse says, "As a result, many of them believed" (v. 12). Because of their nobleness in seeking the truth, the Bereans were able to develop a reasoning that led to belief in the message Paul and Silas gave them. They were able to reconcile one set of information they already knew with another set of information that Paul and Silas gave them. This represents a principle we can still use to this day. Even though we are not trying to reconcile scriptural prophecies with the message of the death, burial, and resurrection of Jesus, the principle outlined in Acts 17 gives us hope that God can lead us through the discernment process in our information-saturated world.

Another principle we can adhere to is using caution before subscribing to the easiest or most comfortable stance, especially when we have not examined multiple perspectives. The competing worlds of information should not lead us into a "filter bubble," but rather incline us to respect the information at hand and discern the perspective that fits with our value systems. Ultimately, unless we are rooting ourselves in the light of Jesus to help us illuminate some of the darkness of our media ecosystems, we will never be fulfilled.

The Verdict

John, in his gospel, draws on motifs and wording from Genesis such as life, light, and darkness. Using this background, John sets Jesus as the light who is brought into the darkness. This light (Jesus) illuminates the darkness and brings knowledge and purity to it as it displays the presence of God.[30]

Everyone encounters inevitable darkness in their lives. This may come in the form of suffering, idolatry, disobedience, or other forms. Everyone's journey out of darkness is different, but we know that Jesus is the light of us all (John 1:4), guiding us to an illuminated life in the presence of God.

But as each of us consider our journeys out of darkness, we must also consider patches of darkness that may still be present in our lives. Not many people I know like to be indicted of wrongdoings, especially in society today, where accusations and seeing the worst in others is so prevalent. Nonetheless, several people I know like critical wisdom on how to follow Jesus better or to recognize roadblocks or blind spots along the way in their faith journeys. Blind spots are called such because you don't know they are there; they can only be discovered by external means, like the means of using multiple mirrors when driving a car. One of my motivations is to encourage others to try to avoid the blind spot—to not miss out on critical relationships with others.

> This is the verdict: Light has come into the world, but people loved darkness instead of light because their deeds were evil. Everyone who does evil hates the light, and will not come into the light for fear that their deeds will be exposed. But whoever lives by the truth comes into the light, so that it may be seen plainly that what they have done has been done in the sight of God. (John 3:19–21)

The reason for our blindness is that we are hindered not by the light, but against the light. In a similar way, many of us are hindered from truly gaining the perspective of others and learning who they are because we are against them.

Frequently, we are not hindered from learning and understanding because people are against us, but because *we* are against *them*. We are more prone to judge other groups by the mistakes of one or just a few, but elevate ourselves based on our good intentions. This can lead us to disengagement with others because of generalizations. We need to step into the example of Jesus and the life that he lived out by *actively* engaging others, including and especially others who are different from us. When we do this—when we see the beauty of God's created people through their histories and their stories—we see a bigger picture of God. We are called to more. Jesus is the judge and the verdict.

As we continue in this endeavor to understand others, we also need to recognize the effects of the environment we live in. As mentioned before, our fractured media ecosystems likely play a role in the way we relate to others, which hinders our ability to understand them. It's easy for us to get blinded by other obstructions. One way to understand our current communication environment better is to understand how we got there.

A Very Brief History of Public Communication and Opinion

Humans have been communicating since we were first created; God gave us the gift of communication. Some early key developments in human communication were cave drawings, Egyptian hieroglyphs, and writing on stone tablets.

Philosophy also had an impact on human communication and public opinion. The Greek philosophers Socrates, Plato, and Aristotle heavily influenced western philosophy and many of the things we understand today. Socrates publicly debated others, and Aristotle created one of the first institutions featuring a research library. In contrast, Plato described Sophists—people who charged residents a fee to teach them methods of persuasion through rhetoric to influence members of society.[31] This was common in Greek politics at the time. A philosopher named Isocrates (not to be confused with Socrates) actually wrote a speech, "Against the Sophists," in which he detailed the failings of some Sophists and how they charged for teaching rhetorical tricks instead of actual principles.[32] Does this sound familiar?

Several developments later, perhaps the most impactful development and greatest influence on communication was Johannes Gutenberg's creation of the printing press. Gutenberg revolutionized printing production, making documents at a lower cost and higher volumes, which resulted in a dramatic increase in people's ability to access knowledge and information.[33] Some people argue that Gutenberg's invention was the most important in human history. Before the printing press revolutionized access to knowledge and information, letters and books had to be copied by hand, which could take months. Not many written materials were available to the general public, so knowledge and information was limited mostly to the elite and to those who could afford to have a hand-copied version of a document.

Probably the most critical development was that Gutenberg's printing press allowed for mass production of the Bible. This resulted in wider-spread biblical literacy, which likely facilitated the Protestant Reformation. The advent of the printing press likely paved the way for some of the most important developments in church history and theology.

Transitioning into the nineteenth century, the invention of many new forms of communication emerged. Samuel Morse invented the telegraph in the 1830s; Alexander Graham Bell invented the telephone in 1876; Thomas Edison invented the phonograph in 1877; and Guglielmo Marconi invented long-distance radio communication circa 1900; along with several other inventions by other inventors. All of these inventions played critical roles in the dynamics of communication.

Another key modern development that has impacted the world like never before is the internet. The internet has contributed to the globalization of the world on a massive scale, through the rapid exchange of information and ideas. It has brought the world closer together—not physically (nor, as we have discussed, intellectually), but in respect to increased levels of communication. People on opposite ends of the earth can exchange emails, instant messages, video calls, and more in a matter of seconds or minutes. There are only a handful of places in the world where the internet is not available. The dawn of the internet created a social tangibility in which people could easily take part. With the ability to now create web pages that could be seen by any other user, communication became simpler and information became more available. News outlets not only participated in using the internet as a way to get their message across; many news outlets were created via only digital formats. In addition, individuals were given avenues to public opinion. Blogs, videos, chat rooms, discussion boards, comment sections on news websites, and especially the onset of social media platforms such as Facebook gave users a way for their voices to be heard.

It seems as though, before the advent of the internet, digital, and social media, the only forms of public communication and opinion were either publicly addressing a crowd through audible voice, protesting or gathering with a group of people to make opinions known, or through writing an opinion piece in a newspaper (which likely still had to be filtered through an editor). What makes the internet and social media unique in regard to public communication and opinion is that if someone wants their thoughts to be known to others, it is easier than ever before to make it happen.

During the late twentieth century, the internet became a sensation, partly because it provided communication that was faster than ever through electronic mail (email). During the same time, blogs were conceived, providing a way for people to communicate anything they wanted and share with whomever they wanted. Into the twenty-first century, social media began to take its place as a principle form of communication and networking. A few years into the rise of social media, Facebook became the go-to site to connect with friends and to share posts with everyone who was a "friend."

How Communication Affects Our Relationships

Through platforms like Facebook, blogs, YouTube, and other avenues of sharing to the public, we now have extremely valuable ways to share our gifts and ideas. However, as great a benefit as these platforms can be, they can also be weaponized. Most of us have probably witnessed comment sections on social media sites that leave us feeling like there is no hope left in humanity. We wonder things like "How can these people be so naive?" "Did they even read the article?" "Why are people so hurtful with their words?" "Why do people spend their time trolling comment sections when no one's mind is ever changed?"

Because of this ability to make our opinions public, somehow we are led to believe that we can also claim exclusive truth to our *opinions* even if they are just grounded in hearsay or no factual knowledge at all. The reinforcement received from other like-minded users through affirmative comments and "likes" propels this further. This can lead to continual carelessness in our stewardship of the internet; and because of this carelessness, we become more and more desensitized to what meaningful dialogue is. In this process, typing behind a computer screen rarely, if ever, leads to good discussions and desirable outcomes. And as much as emojis have helped in offsetting the monotone feeling of typed messages, we still struggle to respectfully engage others over computer screens.

Through this, we risk the devaluing of personal and intentional relationships, which ultimately leads to a lack of perspective. I can't tell you how many times I have been devastated reading comment sections on Facebook from people who seem to have no value for others' thoughts or ideas. It's even more saddening to see that several people leading the way with these types of comments identify as Christian.

The internet is probably not ever going away, so we must strive to find better ways to engage each other in civil dialogue and hear each other's perspectives without the antipathetic rhetoric. I once saw a video of two dogs barking ferociously at each other with a sliding glass door in between them, but when the door was opened, the dogs immediately stopped their loud barking and acted like they were cool with each other. The caption of the video was something along the line of, "This is how people act on social media." I agreed with that assessment.

Usually, the online narratives are framed as "us versus them" and "good versus evil." The rallying narratives behind these arguments are extremely evident, and many of our communication styles on social media produce quick-draw responses and eye-for-eye remarks. We incoherently miss the original points people were trying to make because we are blinded by our original and predisposed beliefs.

We must learn to see perspective even when it's hard. The challenge at hand is not sacrificing thoughts or beliefs you have truly vetted or prayed about, but having the ability to retain those beliefs while respectfully listening and respectfully responding to others who share different views, rather than falling victim to the binary posture of social media discussions. As Christians, let's work to represent ourselves well in media, and let's take responsibility for where we may have been wrong.

Discussion

1. How do you stay informed on current events? What is your information-gathering method? How do you filter through much of the bias that is out there?

2. What responsibility do you think Christians have when it comes to media consumption and interpretation?

3. How does the information you gather about certain events or topics shape the way you view others?

4. Have you ever taken a step back to analyze if the information you are taking in is based more on emotion and hyperbolic rhetoric than on actual facts? How can you better ensure that you're taking in truthful information?

5. Have comments or posts you have made through your social media platform ever hurt any of your relationships? How do you think others view your overall social media presence?

6. How you can use your social media platform in healthy, instead of harmful, ways?

CHAPTER 4

DIVINE CONTACT:
HOW JESUS SHAPES THE REASON
AND THE WAY WE ENGAGE OTHERS

There are two levels to view how Jesus engaged people with contact. In the first level, Jesus engaged others with contact through his ministry on earth. He healed the sick, prescribed perspective to the ruling authorities, told parables about how to treat and love others, and engaged with sinners and outcasts. Jesus' life and ministry on earth provide us with a healthy description and example of how to engage people in our own cultures with intentional contact, which ultimately results in a greater love, respect, and empathy for our neighbors.

We can view the second level in which Jesus engages people with contact from a broader, redemptive perspective. From a theological standpoint, Jesus came to earth incarnate to engage humanity, by reconciling the broken relationship between God and his people. In simple terms, when we enter into a relationship with Jesus—*when we come into contact with Jesus*—we are reconciled to God. And because Jesus stepped into our culture to come in contact with us to heal us and save us, we are also called to step into other cultures and come in contact with people. The earthly and redemptive examples of Jesus compel us to follow him in this way.

God's Perspective

How can we better understand how God sees humanity? We will never be able to fully understand God's perspective because he is infinite and we are finite. However, we can glean from Scripture about the character of God, to help us develop a deeper perspective of humanity. We can't fully understand God until we try to see the world and humanity from his perspective and through his lens. We do this by learning from the example of Jesus.

When we lack the perspective of God, or stop trying to understand the perspective of God, it's much more difficult to make sense of the world and the people around us. With this in mind, our ability to understand others well should be rooted in our ability and our desire to understand God. When we understand God more, we understand his people better; and when we understand people better, we continue to build on the knowledge we have of God because he is the Creator of all people.

Jesus gives us an in-depth look at what it means to understand and engage others. As we follow the example of Jesus, let's think about people in our own lives that we can engage.

Jesus and Nicodemus

Have you ever been the outcast in a group you were a part of? In John 3, we witness the account of Nicodemus' interaction with Jesus that sets him as the outcast among his peers. Nicodemus shows us how being the outcast—as one who wanted to question Jesus personally—may have led him to a greater understanding of whom Jesus was.

It was nighttime when Nicodemus approached Jesus, to question him about everything he had been teaching and the signs he had been performing. His nighttime approach could have meant that he didn't want the other Pharisees knowing that he was visiting Jesus; but even if that wasn't exactly the case, his approach to Jesus still set him apart from the rest of the Jewish ruling authorities—because it seemed that Nicodemus was set on learning something from Jesus.

He likely already knew who Jesus really was because he refers to him as "Rabbi" which denoted respect, especially since Jesus did not have formal rabbinic training. He also acknowledged that God must be with Jesus because of the signs Jesus had been performing. We don't know *exactly* what Nicodemus' intentions were with Jesus, but from the scripture given, it seems he was intentionally seeking after God. It is also interesting to note that at the beginning of their dialogue, Nicodemus doesn't really *ask* Jesus a question before Jesus begins explaining spiritual rebirth to him:

> Jesus replied, "Very truly I tell you, no one can see the kingdom of God unless they are born again."

> "How can someone be born when they are old?" Nicodemus asked. "Surely they cannot enter a second time into their mother's womb to be born!"

> Jesus answered, "Very truly I tell you, no one can enter the kingdom of God unless they are born of water and the Spirit. Flesh gives birth to flesh, but the Spirit gives birth to spirit. You should not be surprised at my saying, 'You must be born again.' The wind blows wherever it pleases. You hear its sound, but you cannot tell where it comes from or where it is going. So it is with everyone born of the Spirit."

> "How can this be?" Nicodemus asked.

"You are Israel's teacher," said Jesus, "and do you not understand these things? Very truly I tell you, we speak of what we know, and we testify to what we have seen, but still you people do not accept our testimony. I have spoken to you of earthly things and you do not believe; how then will you believe if I speak of heavenly things? No one has ever gone into heaven except the one who came from heaven—the Son of Man. Just as Moses lifted up the snake in the wilderness, so the Son of Man must be lifted up, that everyone who believes may have eternal life in him." (John 3:3–15)

Is Jesus really the prophesied savior Nicodemus had been reading about for so long? As a Pharisee, Nicodemus was also rightfully committed to the Law. So when there was a potential threat to the order of the Law—like a guy claiming to be the savior of the world and upending the outwardly liturgical Jewish environment at the time—questions were raised.

In their exchange, Jesus and Nicodemus discuss the need for spiritual rebirth. Jesus taught Nicodemus what it means to be "born again." Nicodemus didn't initially understand what Jesus meant, so he continued to explain how one should be born of water and the Spirit—a reference to spiritual cleansing and being made new through spiritual rebirth, which Jesus likely derived from Ezekiel 36:25–27: "I will sprinkle clean water on you, and you will be clean. . . . I will give you a new heart. . . . And I will put my Spirit in you." This seems to be the case, because Nicodemus was seemingly still confused as to what Jesus was saying, while Jesus questioned how Nicodemus, a teacher of Israel, still didn't understand these things.

In the same context of Scripture, with Jesus still in teaching mode and in part of the larger dialogue with Nicodemus, we find one of the most famous single-verse summaries of the gospel: "For

God so loved the world that he gave his one and only Son, that whoever believes in him shall not perish but have eternal life" (John 3:16). If I am putting myself in the place of Nicodemus and hearing Jesus teach such a powerful message right in front of me, it's hard to imagine that his words would not have an effect on me. That sort of contact with Jesus is powerful, and it's the same contact with Jesus we still have access to today through Scripture.

Leading up to the crucifixion of Jesus, we witness Nicodemus again in John 7 when the chief priests and the Pharisees were calling for the arrest of Jesus. Nicodemus speaks up for Jesus, saying, "Does our law judge a man without first giving him a hearing and learning what he does?" To which they replied, "Are you from Galilee too?" (John 7:51–52)—implying that Nicodemus sympathized with Jesus.

Shortly after Jesus' death, we witness Joseph of Arimathea ask the permission of Pilate to take the body of Jesus—along with Nicodemus, who brought a mixture of myrrh and aloes and bound Jesus' body in linen clothes with the spices for a proper and customary Jewish burial. What happened to Nicodemus along the way that he would stick up for Jesus and also want to honor Jesus with a proper burial?

Nicodemus' contact with Jesus may have given him the understanding and perspective he needed to fully commit to Jesus, whether it was listening to his teachings during their conversation about spiritual rebirth or at a different point along the way. We can deduce that because of the contact Nicodemus had with Jesus, the result was that Nicodemus ultimately followed Jesus.

This serves as a powerful story about what contact with Jesus can do to us. For Nicodemus, although it seemed he was already considering Jesus prior to his conversation and likely didn't completely depart from his Pharisaical way of life during Jesus' time, it still must have taken a lot for him to sympathize with Jesus and desire for him to have a proper Jewish burial.

Sometimes for us, it may take powerful and intentional contact with Jesus, like Nicodemus had, for us to separate ourselves from practices or ways of life that don't follow his example. The Pharisees were doing what they knew and thought was right, following the law. Frequently we too think we are doing the right thing or that our intentions are good, but we also need to see Jesus when he is right in front of us.

Jesus and the Parable of the Good Samaritan

What does it mean to help those in need and come in contact with people even if they are different from us? What if they are from a different culture, socioeconomic status, or ethnicity? Jesus explores what it means to love and how love can transcend these and other categories that separate us.

In his parable of the good Samaritan, Jesus shows us what true contact with others looks like, as he responds to a question raised by an expert in the law: "Who is my neighbor?"

> On one occasion an expert in the law stood up to test Jesus. "Teacher," he asked, "what must I do to inherit eternal life?"
>
> "What is written in the Law?" he replied. "How do you read it?"
>
> He answered, "'Love the Lord your God with all your heart and with all your soul and with all your strength and with all your mind' and, 'Love your neighbor as yourself.'"
>
> "You have answered correctly," Jesus replied. "Do this and you will live."

But he wanted to justify himself, so he asked Jesus, "And who is my neighbor?"

In reply Jesus said: "A man was going down from Jerusalem to Jericho, when he was attacked by robbers. They stripped him of his clothes, beat him and went away, leaving him half dead. A priest happened to be going down the same road, and when he saw the man, he passed by on the other side. So too, a Levite, when he came to the place and saw him, passed by on the other side. But a Samaritan, as he traveled, came where the man was; and when he saw him, he took pity on him. He went to him and bandaged his wounds, pouring on oil and wine. Then he put the man on his own donkey, brought him to an inn and took care of him. The next day he took out two denarii and gave them to the innkeeper. 'Look after him,' he said, 'and when I return, I will reimburse you for any extra expense you may have.'

"Which of these three do you think was a neighbor to the man who fell into the hands of robbers?"

The expert in the law replied, "The one who had mercy on him."

Jesus told him, "Go and do likewise." (Luke 10:25–37)

The implications of this parable of Jesus are deep and wide. We even have "Good Samaritan" laws in our society named after this parable because of the high ethical standards Jesus laid out about helping those in need. However, it's more than just high ethical standards that we take away from Jesus' teaching here. This parable not only teaches us about "who is my neighbor," or having mercy on those in need, but it teaches us the deeply rooted capacities we have to try to justify ourselves by constantly questioning, "Who is my neighbor?"—which sometimes really means, "Who deserves my love or my help?"

In this parable, Jesus is speaking to a Jewish audience. Jews did not have anything to do with Samaritans, who were the disenfranchised and social outcasts at the time. So Jesus explains this parable in a way that cuts deep into the ideological perceptions of the Jewish expert who, differing from Nicodemus, was not approaching Jesus here to learn but to justify himself.

Jesus' parable upends the expert's ideological system by commending the Samaritan as the person who helps the man attacked on the side of the road. To the Jews' perspective, Samaritans were largely viewed as incapable of doing good deeds because of their historical relationship with the Jews. Jesus frames the story in a way that not only puts the Samaritan in the place of the one who had mercy on the attacked, but also when Jesus says, "Go and do likewise," he places the expert and the Samaritan on the same level. The expert is not any more capable of helping those in need than the Samaritan; likewise, the Samaritan is not any more capable than the expert.

There are a variety of valuable viewpoints and allegories through which we can view the parable of the Good Samaritan. But when we think about the parable in terms of not just helping others in need but placing ourselves in the place of the social downtrodden and outcasts and *still* helping others in need, we are able to understand more fully how social standing, race, income level, and more are all transcended by the love of God that compels us to love others. Miroslav Volf states it this way: "At the core of the Christian faith lies the persuasion that the 'others' need not be perceived as innocent in order to be loved, but ought to be embraced even when they are perceived as wrongdoers."[34]

Despite the animosity between the Jews and the Samaritans, Jesus uses this story to show that both groups need each other and can help each other. Those we may view as the social "other" may actually have something to give us and teach us, just as Jesus uses the Samaritan to teach the Jewish expert what it meant to love his neighbor. Jesus used this story of contact between the Samaritan and the beaten traveler to exemplify that there is no "other" in the realm of the kingdom of God. We are all capable of loving others, no matter how different they may be from us. Where are we afraid of contact with those we are different from, or whom we may perceive as wrongdoers? It's easy for our own cultures to make us feel worlds apart from other cultures, just as the expert probably thought the Samaritans were worlds apart and in completely different value dimensions. Certainly they were worlds apart when it came to culture and social standing, but not when it came to loving well and helping others.

What type of people are you distanced from, intentionally or unintentionally? Immigrants, other races and ethnicities, political affiliations? Jesus shares this parable to answer the question of "Who is my neighbor?" to reveal to us that love transcends all categories that may separate us as human beings.

Quick to Listen, Slow to Speak

We have much to learn from the *way* Jesus conversed with others, but also a lot to glean from *whom* he conversed with. The brother of Jesus, James, discusses in his epistle what it means to communicate in a healthy way with others, by emphasizing listening and minimizing speaking too quickly. This is significant because when we are communicating with others who hold different thoughts or opinions, speaking over them minimizes the value of what they are trying to communicate, while idolizing one's own thoughts or opinions as superior. James tells us to be careful of this, because it can result in anger that produces unrighteousness.

> My dear brothers and sisters, take note of this: Everyone should be quick to listen, slow to speak and slow to become angry, because human anger does not produce the righteousness that God desires. Therefore, get rid of all moral filth and the evil that is so prevalent and humbly accept the word planted in you, which can save you. (James 1:19–21)

This may be one of the most applicable pieces of advice in the book of James, given the current social climate we live in today. The book of James is one of the most unique writings in the New Testament. It is not a narrative-style book like the four gospel collections, neither is it a letter to a specific church correcting, encouraging, or rebuking them like Paul's epistles. James is more like the Old Testament book of Proverbs, a collection of sayings and teachings that really aren't in any particular order. It is written to first-century Jewish Christians scattered throughout the region who are experiencing various trials and persecution, and this is the context in which we should read James.

You have probably heard similar sayings along this continuum such as, "seek to understand before being understood," or "listen more, talk less." At root, these sayings are great advice if they are understood in the way James was describing how we should be quick to listen and slow to speak. It's very interesting, though, that James doesn't just emphasize listening, but emphasizes listening *first*. What if we applied this principle to our lives?

Our ability to listen is related to our desire to speak, and is also related to our anger. When I think about all the anger and outrage in the world today, I think about how much of it could be diffused if people actively listened first before acting.

Ed Stetzer, in his book *Christians in the Age of Outrage*, describes several well-known events that resulted in nonsensical escalation due to miscommunication, people jumping to quick conclusions, and people not listening first. His initial thesis of the book is that some Christians have actually contributed to the state of outrage in our society by promoting, instead of dismantling, silly ideas and conspiracies, largely because they have not taken the time to investigate and *listen* for themselves to what is actually going on, because "outrage overwhelms truth."[35] But it doesn't have to.

This follows the progression that James describes in verses 19–20. When we are slow to listen, then we are quick to speak and quick to become angry, and this results in an unrighteous anger that is not desirable by God. "Righteousness" can also be closely translated as "justice." When we are slow to listen, quick to speak, and quick to become angry, we are actually doing *injustice* to those to whom we ought to be listening.

Think about how you can practically apply this principle in your own life. How can we emphasize listening as a way to enhance our conversations that will contribute to relationships developed around understanding?

Culture Disrupted

God is responsible for the diversity of humans, and it's perhaps one of God's greatest gifts to us. Like a painting, we all represent different shades and different details of his creation and we all contribute to the beauty of his creation as a whole. God's creation of people of different ethnicities, languages, nationalities, etc., produces richly distinct and valuable cultures all over the world. This gift of culture can teach us not only more about his people, but more about him. The diversity of different cultures creates a unique opportunity for Christians to love God and love our neighbors in ways that we may have never thought.

When God created the world, he also created culture as a context of human flourishing so that we can work toward its redemption and enjoy its goodness.[36] When God created man and woman, there existed a perfect culture of human and divine relationship. God created Adam and Eve and their descendants with elements of culture that included marriage and family, work and stewardship of the earth's resources, leisure, food, and more.[37] There was a shared understanding and a way of life that God instituted.

God lived in unbroken contact with the first humans, until Adam and Eve disobeyed God. They were deceived into thinking they could become like God. This is the moment when contact was broken. God, in his character, could no longer live in union with humankind because of their disobedience and sin. But God also, in his love and righteousness, immediately offered a path forward. In Genesis 3:15, God offers the promise of a savior: "he will crush your head, and you will strike his heel."

In their sin, God also covers Adam and Eve's nakedness with cloth from an animal. This is foreshadowing imagery: Jesus would also act as the sacrificial lamb to cover the sin of all those who believe in him. It is in these moments that God offers a way to mend the broken contact.

Heaven on Earth

This, then, is how you should pray:
"Our Father in heaven,
hallowed be your name,
your kingdom come,
your will be done,
on earth as it is in heaven.
Give us today our daily bread.
And forgive us our debts,

as we also have forgiven our debtors.

And lead us not into temptation,

but deliver us from the evil one." (Matt. 6:9–13, emphasis added)

We often discuss what will be in heaven and what won't be. We ask questions like, "Will we still be married in heaven?" "Will there be animals in heaven?" "Will heaven have sports or other forms of entertainment?" "Will we get hungry in heaven and have food?" or "Will there be some of my favorite items from earth in heaven?" Many of these questions are often rooted in people's personal desires of what they want heaven to be like.

The glimpses of heaven we get in Revelation, in contrast, consist of a continual exaltation and worship of God. Take a quick read through Revelation 4 to gain a better picture of the way John describes his vision of heaven:

> After this I looked, and there before me was a door standing open in heaven. And the voice I had first heard speaking to me like a trumpet said, "Come up here, and I will show you what must take place after this." At once I was in the Spirit, and there before me was a throne in heaven with someone sitting on it. And the one who sat there had the appearance of jasper and ruby. A rainbow that shone like an emerald encircled the throne. Surrounding the throne were twenty-four other thrones, and seated on them were twenty-four elders. They were dressed in white and had crowns of gold on their heads. From the throne came flashes of lightning, rumblings and peals of thunder. In front of the throne, seven lamps were blazing. These are the seven spirits of God. Also in front of

the throne there was what looked like a sea of glass, clear as crystal.

In the center, around the throne, were four living creatures, and they were covered with eyes, in front and in back. The first living creature was like a lion, the second was like an ox, the third had a face like a man, the fourth was like a flying eagle. Each of the four living creatures had six wings and was covered with eyes all around, even under its wings. Day and night they never stop saying:

"Holy, holy, holy is the Lord God Almighty, who was, and is, and is to come."

Whenever the living creatures give glory, honor and thanks to him who sits on the throne and who lives forever and ever, the twenty-four elders fall down before him who sits on the throne and worship him who lives for ever and ever. They lay their crowns before the throne and say:

"You are worthy, our Lord and God, to receive glory and honor and power, for you created all things, and by your will they were created and have their being." (Rev. 4:1–11)

It's tempting to read sections of Scripture like this and think to ourselves, "Heaven actually seems kind of boring," although no professing Christian would ever admit that. But it is this underlying nuance that drives us to ask the questions above, because we think that there has to be more to heaven than just worshipping, right? I mean, we all love worshipping at church, but there's no way we would like singing all day and all night. The truth is that the more our perspective is shaped into an eternal perspective through the lens of God, the more we come to realize that heaven is a place where we are no longer battling for our sanctification but now are able to live in our glorification. And because of this, our purest desire is to constantly worship and praise the Creator. We can only assume what will and will not be in heaven by what evidence there is in Scripture. We don't know exactly what heaven will be like and what exactly will be there, but there are a few things we can be certain about. For one, we know that we take our ethnicity with us and that heaven will be a multicultural experience. Ultimately, heaven will be a unique blending of ethnicities to create a unified culture of God.

> After this I looked, and there before me was a great multitude that no one could count, from every nation, tribe, people and language, standing before the throne and before the Lamb. They were wearing white robes and were holding palm branches in their hands. (Rev. 7:9)

The true essence of heaven is worshipping God, and we know that such an experience will consist of people from every ethnōs (ἔθνους). So how do we apply a heaven-on-earth perspective with this scriptural truth? If we are seeking this perspective and are under the understanding that heaven will be a diverse and multicultural worship experience, should we not long for the same reality while we are here on earth, like Jesus taught his disciples to pray? If you aren't open to and don't love diversity here on earth, your expectations of heaven aren't going to be met, because heaven will be the most diverse experience you will ever encounter.

Integration is a key step to building a more complete perspective of heaven on earth. In heaven, there will be no isolation of different ethnic groups, nor will there be domination by a select few ethnic groups. We will all be fully and equally integrated into the kingdom of God, praising his name as one collective heavenly culture.

As related earlier, I've been blessed enough to get a glimpse of this while volunteering with a refugee ministry in Greece. Each night we would gather for worship in what was a profound experience that really felt like a taste of heaven. The majority of the camp were Afghan and Iranian refugees, along with several volunteers from a variety of countries. I remember worshipping with all of them and thinking to myself, "This is what heaven will be like." It was one of the most surreal experiences I have ever had and I know that I have even more to look forward to—because as beautiful as the diverse worship experience was, it won't compare to our actual experience in heaven.

Out of all the traits and characteristics John could have recognized in his vision of heaven, he recognized the unique diversity of "every tribe, every tongue, every nation." As we continue to move toward a heaven-on-earth perspective, let us not grow weary of or misuse diversity in political arenas. Instead, let's love diversity, because it shows the creativity of God and gives us a glimpse of heaven.

Discussion

1. Describe your contact moment(s) with Jesus. How does your contact with him continue?

2. Can you relate to Nicodemus in the way that he encountered Jesus? In what ways?

3. What type of people have you encountered in your life that you may have deemed unworthy of help in light of your perception of them? Read Jesus' parable of the Good Samaritan. What does it truly mean to not just love your neighbor, but to recognize who your neighbor is?

4. Can you think of an instance in your life where you were initially outraged by an issue or someone else's viewpoint, but upon listening you began to understand it better? How can you apply this principle of *listening first* in different areas of your life?

5. What is your initial view of what heaven will be like? How can John's description of his vision of heaven help shape our thoughts and actions with people from different cultural groups?

CHAPTER 5

PERSPECTIVES, STORIES, AND CASE STUDIES

When we take the time to observe the concept of contact, we more readily recognize many accounts in which it is already working. This chapter will examine several real-life examples where contact has changed lives and broadened perspectives, as well as several initiatives that have attempted to breed intentional interaction between people who are different.

There is power in hearing people's stories. There is power in hearing how contact has changed people's lives. My hope is that you'll listen to some of these powerful and practical examples and be motivated and encouraged to seek out a person or a group of a different status or viewpoint, truly learn why they share that difference, and learn how to better understand them as people created in the image of God.

Solution Sunday

There have been several events in the US in recent years that have induced a range of emotions from a variety of different Americans.

Perhaps some of the most intense emotions revolve around the deaths of black men at the hands of white police officers. The mere reading of a subject like that can spark emotions of outrage, empathy, anger, confusion, apathy, fatigue, and more. Although there is no way to completely feel and understand the emotions of a family or community who lost a loved one, it seems that the emotions of these families and communities are rooted in wanting to know the truth and longing for justice.

These communities don't need statistics about their interactions with white law enforcement officials; they know something seems off because of the stories they hear from their friends and neighbors about a simple traffic stop, because of the videos they have seen, or because several of them have faced hostilities themselves. The media has covered stories about the deaths of these men and the ensuing protests in a variety of ways, some presenting the situations as a reason for police reform, others generalizing the protests as overexaggerations.

In July of 2016, in response to the growing racial tensions, senators James Lankford of Oklahoma and Tim Scott of South Carolina proposed a simple and practical solution that could have a profound impact. In a joint article they published in *Time Magazine*, in the aftermath of the shooting of eight police officers in Dallas and the deaths of two black men in Baton Rouge and St. Paul, the senators challenged the narrative that made many people feel like they had to choose between supporting the police or supporting Americans upset by the deaths of the two black men.

Senator Lankford, who is white, and Senator Scott, who is black, proposed a better way forward to understand and cope with some of the racial tensions in the country: "We must start by realizing that our personal perspectives are different."[38] They acknowledged that the police have dangerous jobs and offer a sacrifice in their daily work, but also acknowledged that many blacks constantly feel stereotyped and suspiciously judged by some law enforcement officers.[39]

The senators went on to describe how community leaders and legislators often propose policy to address "police and criminal justice reform, racial reconciliation, mental illness, a seemingly growing culture of violence, and jobs."[40] They also acknowledged that while the role of government is important in many situations, it can't solve every issue, and that "this is also an issue of trust that exists in the hearts of millions of people. Trust can only be built by spending time together and getting to know one another."[41]

Senators Lankford and Scott recognized that spending intentional time with people who are different than ourselves, and outside our normal communities, creates an avenue to build trust and gain perspective. They proposed an idea they called "Solution Sunday":

> Americans do not really get to know their neighbors and fellow citizens at a rally or a big event, we get to know each other typically over a meal, especially in our home. What if Americans intentionally chose to put our prejudice and broken trust on the table by putting our feet under the same table? If it seems too simple and obvious, let me ask you this question . . . have you ever had dinner in your home with a person of another race? Many Americans have not. Sunday is a slower, yet significant day, for most Americans. So, we challenge each family to give one Sunday lunch or dinner for building relationships across race, to literally be part of the solution in America. Obviously any day of the week works since the goal is to engage on the personal level of your own home to break down walls and build trust across our communities. It is harder to stereotype when you know people first-hand.[42]

Senators Lankford and Scott described how their own personal relationship has developed and prospered. Even though they are from different states, backgrounds, races, and cultures and have some differing political opinions, they are friends and respect each other. We all can learn from senator Lankford and Scott. As the world, and the US, becomes more globalized and we encounter people from different backgrounds and cultures, we must be active in getting to know people intentionally. Solution Sunday suggests that we can take part in contact—intentionally getting to know others who are different from ourselves. It is this kind of example that can help us see the value, and the results, of a white man and a black man getting to know each other. The hope is that implementing ideas like Solution Sunday in our communities will lead to new and renewed perspectives that will also lead to an understanding of the broken systems in our world, and will catalyze us to turn toward justice in the world.

How Can You Hate Me if You Don't Even Know Me?

Perhaps one of the most intriguing examples of contact at work is the life and story of Daryl Davis, a black blues musician who spends his time befriending members of the Ku Klux Klan (KKK). When approaching members of the KKK, Davis takes a gentle yet intelligent approach. He calmly confronts them with the question, "How can you hate me if you don't even know me?"[43]

In a podcast interview, Davis described his first encounter with a member of the KKK. It was 1983 and Davis was playing a show with his band at an all-white venue in Frederick, MD. After their set, he was approached by a man complimenting him on his piano skills. The man said, "I'd never heard a black pianist play like Jerry Lee Lewis," to which Davis replied, "Who do you think taught Jerry Lee Lewis to play that way?"[44]

Following some more conversation, Davis observed that this man had never conversed with a black man before, which led Davis to ask why. "I'm a member of the Ku Klux Klan," the man replied. Davis thought he was joking, but the man proceeded to pull out his Klan card from his pocket as proof.[45] This sparked a movement, by Davis's own volition, that led him to begin befriending members of the KKK in attempts to lead them out of such darkness by getting to know him as a human being and not only as a black man.

> The most important thing I learned is that when you are actively learning about someone else you are passively teaching them about yourself. . . . Give them a platform. You challenge them. But you don't challenge them rudely or violently. You do it politely and intelligently. And when you do things that way chances are they will recip-rocate and give you a platform.[46]

There are several things Davis emphasizes here. One is learning. Truly diving into someone's life, thoughts, desires, struggles, relationships, background, culture, and more is the path to understanding them; at the same time, they begin to understand you. Davis's intention in building relationships with members of the KKK was to challenge them with a different perspective, a process driven by learning.

I think one issue that we face, and that many Christians struggle with, is learning about those who come from different backgrounds. Like myself, many people grow up and live within many monocultural spheres in their lives, whether it's family, school, work, church, or neighborhood. We have to actively seek out relationships with those we don't understand, but we also have to *desire* to want to understand them. You may find yourself stating, "I just don't know why that group of people thinks they are correct on this issue," or asking, "Why in the world would that person ever think she is right about this topic?" At the same time, you might hear people say things like, "Things are just so divisive these days," or "I don't understand why our country is so polarized." It's likely because we rarely tax ourselves when it comes to actively trying to learn the perspectives of those we think are the ones being divisive.

The other thing Davis emphasizes is the polite and genuine tone he takes in his attempt at discourse. As highlighted previously, the current state of discourse that many people take, including many Christians, is harmful and counterproductive to actually learning perspectives and solving issues. Even though Davis might completely disagree and even bear anger to what these members of the KKK stand for, he also understands that for there to be any chance for them to get to know him and for them to reciprocate, he must approach them with a tone and politeness that shows he is doing it out of love.

Often when we see or meet people or groups we disagree with, especially on issues that might trigger anger within us (and understandably so in some cases), we are too quick to generalize and force our opinions upon them without truly hearing why they believe what they believe.

One of the most remarkable things about Davis's story is that his attempt at contact with members of the KKK resulted in him gaining a friendship with imperial wizard and white supremacist Roger Kelly. Davis and Kelly's friendship grew, and eventually Kelly quit the Klan and gave up his robe and hood to Davis. Kelly isn't the only former KKK member who has turned in his robe. Davis has several robes from several former members, which he keeps as a way to confront history and as a reminder that talking to Klansmen "has worked for me and I've proven it. . . . I appeal to people's common sense. I don't seek to convert them but if they spend time with me, they can't hate me. [The Klansman] sees that I want the same thing for my family as he does for his. . . . If you can work on the things in common, that's how you build friendship."[47]

Even though not all white people are members of the KKK and carry around an overt hatred for people of color, we can still use the example and success that Davis has shown as a way of listening to our black neighbors and coworkers. Davis's story is threaded with hope that intentionality in relationships is a key to others learning more about you. As Davis puts it, "when you are actively learning about someone else you are passively teaching them about yourself."[48]

Learning to Listen

Austin Hamilton, a white student minister, currently serves in ministry at First Baptist Church Ripley in Ripley, a small and fairly rural town in north Mississippi. Austin recalls his journey to better understanding what it means about coming in contact with others.[49] As a white man, his story is easily relatable to myself and probably so many other white men who grew up in atmospheres that may not have been as conducive to multicultural engagement.

Austin speaks with openness and a strong sense of how far the Lord has brought him in his journey. "I was raised in a community with strong racial barriers in every area of life."

Here, Austin shows great courage in recognizing the deeply rooted sin in himself and his environment that he was brought up in and the effects it had on his attitudes toward minorities.

Austin's description here is similar for many of us. The degrees in which we grow up in environments like this are different for everyone ranging from implicit expressions of racism to very explicit demonstrations. For Austin, his transformative relationship with Jesus and the opportunities that brought him to interact with and understand others different from himself helped him see that no matter what color or background people are from, or even if we perceive them as wrongdoers, Jesus welcomes all.

Austin's process of understanding was influenced by a few events, including being a resident at a church plant in Memphis, TN, where he was able to meet a variety of people, including immigrant workers in the roofing industry. He got to know them, and because of his contact with them, he was able to develop his views from suspicion to love. Austin didn't have an "aha" moment but says, "It was a period of time where I met and listened to others. That is the key—learning to listen rather than talking."

Another powerful aspect of Austin's journey involves his father-in-law, who is white and a pastor at a majority black church and who Austin describes as a gifted and humble leader who has had a formative impact in his life. Austin's journey offered him exposure to building cross-racial friendships through an experience that was not sought out, but just kind of fallen into.

> The year I attended Freedom Fellowship literally changed my whole life. I was so hesitant to go because. . . . I was afraid of something different. I finally attended and was blown away by the freeness of the worship and the Spirit. I also was convicted of my bias blind spots. [The members] loved me so well through it all. I have went back and taught and preached several times. They are a growing church that continues to love the widows and the fatherless with the love of the gospel.

This unique dynamic offered Austin opportunity to truly know different people who shared the common goal of pursuing Christ. His story is encouraging to me because it represents an individual and relatable experience that several of us might understand—someone who came from this type of background, a very small Southern town not conducive to multicultural relationships, with a heritage still struggling to accept and embrace others because of a variety of reasons. But because of God's sovereignty and Austin's relationships with people who grew up differently than he did, he is now in a ministry position where cultural competency is very important and continues to minister to students of all colors, accepting and welcoming them, valuing their differences, all with the collective pursuit of Jesus.

One thing that I have learned in my own journey is that people only act off the information they are surrounded with, and that their beliefs and worldview only go as far as the information they are exposed to. So when we consider people who do not actively engage others or even seem openly hostile to others and devalue their perspectives, it is likely because they are only acting off what they know; they simply don't spend intentional time with people who are different from them. If you get it—if you understand the heavenly benefits of engaging others—share those benefits with people who don't get it yet.

Comfortable at Arm's Length

Derek McClardy, a gifted worship leader, skilled musician, college and young adult minister, and a black man, represents another unique perspective of contact at work in his life. I became friends with Derek in 2016 when I moved to Atlanta. He's taught me a lot about perspective along the way through the circumstances he's been in and the experiences he has grown in throughout his life.

Derek's particular journey to understanding others involves his relationship with white people and his familial background. Derek has a wife who is white, and describes himself as feeling "very comfortable at arm's length" with white people. He grew up in a predominantly white school and church, so he learned how to navigate the culture well along the way. Learning to navigate still came with its challenges and confusions along the way. Although he has positive views of white people, he has still encountered "a number of poor experiences with white culture where [he] felt alienated and out-casted." These are experiences he still wrestles with today.

There are also those experiences that his family cautioned him about while growing up. He describes how he was "taught to be wary of pink people" and how his family mostly hung out with other black friends, possibly as a result of negative experiences with whites. He describes how his culture growing up, and black culture, is generally more collective than white culture. And of course, Derek's family was only looking out for his best interests.

Regardless of Derek's environment growing up and how he may have been influenced to think, he has navigated relationships in ways that show courage and strength, and in ways that majority-culture members have probably never had to deal with. Derek, despite hearing stories from his family and facing challenges that affected him negatively, learned through relationships that it is better to be curious than it is to bear judgment about others, no matter what their skin color.

Without minimizing the negative experiences that others like Derek may have had, we recognize the effort that people like Derek make to continue to build relationships with others of different races. And we recognize the effort we all can make, no matter what our cultural background, to work toward breaking down walls and crossing bridges so that we can understand people better.[50]

The Power of Story and Meals

A vital element of contact is hearing people's stories. Hearing people's stories face to face can evoke emotions in us that we aren't used to. There is a difference between just hearing stories on the news about impoverished communities, racially targeted populations, the plight of immigrants, the persecution of religions, and the agenda of a political party and actually hearing members of groups like these share their personal narratives. Hearing from individuals helps increase our understanding of groups as a whole. When you know someone personally, it's much more difficult to discount their experiences. Additionally, one practical way to carry this out is through sharing meals together.

Several organizations exist to create opportunities for people who normally wouldn't hear each other's stories or share a meal together—Be The Bridge, Narrative 4, Q Ideas, Preemptive Love Coalition, More in Common, Decatur Dinners (for the Atlanta area), and many more. All of these organizations facilitate the sharing of stories and meals; many of them also offer educational and training opportunities that go even deeper. Check out some of these organizations and see if they are organizing events near you or if they have chapters in your city that you can get involved with.

Discussion

1. How do you see the conditions of contact theory playing out in some of these stories?

2. What other stories can you think of where contact was successfully displayed?

3. Is there an organization near you working to break down barriers between groups of people that you could take part in? Would you consider participating in its programming?

CHAPTER 6

UNDERSTANDING CULTURE

Culture

Imagine that you work for an international company that has employees in various regions of the world. There is a business conference being hosted in your city, and several of the international employees are flying in to take part. Since it's in your city of residence, you offer to pick up one of the international employees from their hotel to take to the conference. Your colleague is from the Middle East and he is newer to the company, so this is his first time attending a conference in the US like this. You speak with him the day before and inform him that you will pick him up at 4:30 p.m., just enough time to drive to the conference center where the event begins at 5 p.m.

You show up at the hotel and your colleague opens the door to greet you; likewise, you greet him and shake his hand. You then notice that he doesn't have his shoes on, and something smells like tea brewing in his room. As you begin to think that you need to leave now to make it to the conference on time, your colleague insists that you come in for tea. You kindly decline his offer and instead insist that you need to leave right away because the event is beginning soon. He seems taken aback by your decline of his offer, as you also begin to kindly instruct him to put his shoes on. You explain to him further that you are going to be late for the conference now because he wasn't ready to go at the agreed-upon arrival time. He eventually puts his shoes on and forgoes the tea, and you both make it to the conference only a few minutes late.

You think to yourself how a professional could be so lackluster and unprepared. Conversely, your Middle Eastern colleague is thinking how uptight you are and why you would not want to take a few minutes to take off your shoes and have some tea. This is a classic example of a cultural difference.

Your cultural value is one that represents placing an emphasis on planning and adhering to the scheduled tasks, while your colleague comes from a culture that places value on flexibility and adaptability; it's especially typical to invite guests in for tea or a snack, often regardless of any schedules in play. You may not be actively aware that these are cultural norms that you abide by, but nonetheless, both of your perceived attitudes toward each other are actually just cultural misunderstandings.

When I was working in refugee resettlement as a case manager, a large portion of my job included scheduling appointments for refugees, and picking them up to take them to their appointments because they didn't yet have their own driver's licenses. More often than not, I encountered clients who were not ready at the time I told them and who insisted that I come in for coffee or tea. I would find myself trying to explain the importance of appointments and scheduling in the US and that if we don't make it in time we will have to reschedule. As I continued to learn, perhaps a better way I could have balanced these cultural differences would have been to show up a few minutes earlier so we could have time to chat, but also explaining the importance of keeping and showing up on time for scheduled appointments in the US from a doctor's or other professional's perspective.

Navigating cultural differences in this day and age is more important than ever. Because of this, it is very important that we consider cultural competence and orientation toward difference in our contact with others. Not only does our competence and orientation help us better understand different people before we have a contact moment with them—which makes us more open to their understandings and perspectives—but our competence and orientation also helps us navigate and deepen relationships that we already have.

I would also like to note that I am a student of culture and continually growing and learning. In no way do I have all the knowledge or answers about all things cultural. But I have seen the incredible significance of learning about culture as a positive factor in our relational contact with others, which is why I have included this section.

Defining Culture

The term "culture" is used in a variety of ways and a variety of contexts. We use the term to describe "the characteristic features of everyday existence (such as diversions or a way of life) shared by people in a place or time."[51] In this way, we can think of culture in terms of nationality, ethnicity, region, race, religion, and ideas, just to name a few. We also hear the word "culture" in relation to shared organizational or team structures—"the set of shared attitudes, values, goals, and practices that characterizes an institution or organization."[52] I remember playing sports in high school and the coaches would often refer to improving the team culture, meaning the way we carried ourselves and the patterns of consistent hard work and excellence that they desired the team to have. We hear this in the context of our corporate and business cultures as well.

Often when we think of culture, we think of it as a macro-level subject in terms of race, ethnicity, or nationality. These categories are extremely relevant to the subject of culture as a whole; however, culture is as much a micro-level subject as it is a macro-level one. On a micro level, our nuclear families have distinct cultural behaviors and values that differ from other nuclear families. A simple example of this is when I moved in with a roommate. We began the process of learning how each other does things around the apartment, and we encountered differences because the homes we grew up in and the way our parents taught us to do things were just not the same. When washing dishes, I was taught that it was acceptable to put dishes in the dishwasher even if there was still a small amount of residue from food leftover on the plate; however, my roommate was taught to clean it off well in the sink before putting it into the dishwasher. Is one of us wrong on the way we wash our dishes? (Some of you may think so!) No, we simply recognize the fact that our families had different ways of doing things—a different culture—and that just because they are different and we are not used to it doesn't mean it is wrong. This is a minuscule example of a larger theme of culture, which is: differences do not always mean "wrong."

Other familial cultural values could run deeper, such as holiday celebrations, child rearing, and parental care. Each family is unique in the way they live, and different from the families next door.

Building toward a macro-level view of culture, we continue to identify cultural norms and values that go beyond the familial unit, such as the schools and universities we attend that have different practices, behaviors, and traditions than other schools; or our workplaces, which also have unique cultural norms that differentiate it from others. These are common categories with unique characteristics. We often find ourselves saying or thinking about how our school or university traditions are different from other local or regional schools and universities. Especially in the workplace, when we find ourselves in a new job, it is easy to recognize the key differences, positive or negative, that differentiate the new workplace from our old one. This could range from what we wear to work to how acceptable it is to go five minutes over your lunch break without it being a big deal. Each group that we participate in—whether it's family, school, or work—has its own unique way of doing things: its own culture.

Geographically, we are also members of cultures that represent a distinct and unique way of doing things. For example, culture in the Southern US probably looks a lot different from culture in the New England states. The food, art, dialects, familial values, political leanings, heritage, and traditions are all unique to geographical location.

On a macro level, race, ethnicity, and nationality are all characterized with their own cultures as well. Races within the US represent their own learned behaviors and ideas that bring them together as a collective whole. For our purposes, it's especially important to recognize the distinct experiences and ideas of different cultures in the US and to try to understand, as previously mentioned, that different doesn't always equal "wrong."

On a global level, countries also have their own set of shared belief systems and ways of life that make them different from other countries. Many countries have had traditions for thousands of years. These differences manifest themselves in a variety of ways in lighter things such as food, clothing, art, and language, but also with deeper things like verbal and nonverbal communication, gender roles, religion, negotiation, and more.

Cultural Impacts

Although many features in certain cultures maintain themselves for years and will likely never change, culture is also a dynamic matter that *can* change. Every so often we experience events that cause cultural shifts in our ways of thinking, doing, and the way we see the world—think about events like the civil rights movement; the 1960s space race; the invention of the mobile phone; advancements in DNA testing in criminal cases; the recent refugee crisis; and the advent and widespread use of the internet, social media, and memes (yes, I'm including memes as a cultural impact). All of these events and instances impact culture in different ways.

Culture is everywhere. It impacts who we are, what we do, and how we view the world around us. That is why it is important to understand not just what culture is, but how to read it and how to continue to learn about it. Impactful events like the ones listed are just part of the larger culture they affect and the people who are included in the culture. As we dive deeper into culture, let's examine how to understand people in regard to it.

What Is Cultural Competence?

In the summer of 2014, I spent a few weeks living with a host family in Seville, Spain. They were very hospitable during my stay there, cooking meals, washing my clothes, letting me come and go as I pleased, and more. Toward the end of my stay, I wanted to reciprocate their spirited hospitality so I asked them if they would like me to cook an American-style meal for them and whether there was any specific food they would like. They responded with barbecue, bacon-cheese fries, and sweet tea. Now, being from Mississippi you think I would know exactly how to execute a delicious barbecue meal, but not really. I didn't have access to a grill or smoker or other typical ways of cooking barbecue (not that I really would've known how to at the time anyway), so I did what I usually do when I need to figure something out: I looked it up on Google.

I searched for ways to cook barbecue and concluded that a conventional oven would be the most efficient method. I went to the local market to purchase the meat and returned to cook it early in the afternoon, knowing that it would take a few hours to cook. I remembered that I should cook the pork at about 400–450 degrees; however, when

I was preparing the oven, I noticed that the temperature setting only went up to 225 degrees. I thought to myself, "This must just be a cultural thing and their appliances are different than ours." So I figured I would just cook it at the lower temperature for longer.

Two of my friends came over a little while later to join us for dinner. I informed them that I had already put the pork in the oven and that it would be a while before it was done. I began to explain to one of my friends that it would take longer than expected because the oven only went up to 225 degrees. She then looked confusedly at me, then at the oven, then said, "Tyler, that's 225 degrees Celsius, not Fahrenheit." I felt slightly embarrassed at this cultural gaffe I had just committed, but it was also very laughable. Luckily, the Celsius temperature I had set it at was close enough to the Fahrenheit temperature I had originally intended it to be at anyway, and it turned out great.

This is only a small example of how cultural differences can impact our actions and behavior. Developing cultural competence doesn't necessarily mean knowing the specific characteristics and practices of specific cultures, although that is a part of it. It means being able to modify your actions and behavior to culturally appropriate ways and view everything through the lens of the cultural context you're in.

"Cultural competence" is a broad term that can encompass several different definitions and vocabularies. Terms like cultural intelligence, intercultural competence, intercultural development, cross-cultural competence, cultural adaptation, and cultural humility can all be found in the realm of learning more about cultural understanding. Terminology will continue to shift and grow regarding this subject as it is examined more in various fields and practices. Academic institutions, scholars, and other cultural knowledge or development-based organizations may provide their own definitions. Here are a couple of definitions to grasp a better understanding of some of these terms:

Cross, et al., provides an encompassing definition of cultural competency, including the implications of "culture" and "competence":

> Cultural competence is a set of congruent behaviors, attitudes, and policies that come together in a system, agency, or among professionals and enable that system, agency, or those professionals to work effectively in cross-cultural situations. The word "culture" is used because it implies the integrated pattern of human behavior that includes thoughts, communications, actions, customs, beliefs, values, and institutions of a racial, ethnic, religious, or social group. The word competence is used because it implies having the capacity to function effectively. A culturally competent system of care acknowledges and incorporates—at all levels—the importance of culture, the assessment of cross-cultural relations, vigilance towards the dynamics that result from cultural differences, the expansion of cultural knowledge, and the adaptation of services to meet culturally-unique needs.[53]

The Center for Cultural Intelligence defines cultural intelligence (CQ) as:

> The capability to relate and work effectively in culturally diverse situations. Going beyond existing notions of cultural sensitivity and awareness, it is important to identify the recurring capabilities of individuals who can successfully and respectfully accomplish their objectives, whatever the cultural context. Awareness is the first step, but it's not enough. A culturally intelligent individual is not only aware but can also effectively work and relate with people and projects across different cultural contexts.[54]

The common themes highlighted across these definitions are awareness and acknowledgement of the cultural and social elements at hand, and the capability and knowledge to respond appropriately to those elements. In 2011, cross-cultural competency was ranked as a top-ten skill needed for the future.[55] And even more recently, in 2019, *Forbes* magazine rated cultural intelligence among the top ten job skills that companies are currently looking for in employees.[56]

Settings for cultural competence include domestic and international business, healthcare professions, college and university settings, interethnic relations, and increasingly, churches and other religious organizations. Training in cultural competence in each of these fields is becoming more common. Even so, for US Christians, who begin to encounter more diversity, the need for cultural competence grows—not only for engaging foreign nationals but in order to continue to understand and address the different cultures and cultural trends within America.

Assessing Cultural Competence

Assessing people's or group's cultural competency has become another growing field of study over the last several years. Increasingly, many companies and organizations are choosing to implement tools that assess their employees' and their overall team's cultural competence, since working across cultures is becoming more prevalent as the world continues to globalize. There is a plethora of tools out there that assess cultural competence in different ways. Some tests focus on demographic characteristics and personality traits, while others focus on the degree to which your team is open and ready to explore cultural differences, or your orientation toward the way you engage cultural differences; yet others test unconscious bias or predict cultural adjustment capability.[57] In the end, companies and organizations choose the tool that measures what they value or what they think will benefit them the most.

There are several great organizations dedicated to assessing and improving cultural competence for individuals and organizations. Go Culture International is a research-based company that provides assessment and training tools geared toward expatriates in the areas of business, education, and humanitarian causes. Go Culture's system not only measures cultural competence, but also focuses on leadership and external support factors. Companies like Go Culture are pioneering innovative solutions for people to be adequately prepared for interaction with, or immersion in, other cultures.

Another such organization is Intercultural Development Inventory®, LLC (IDI®). When I referred previously to orientation toward difference, this is the key scientific assessment that measures that. The IDI is a research-based assessment that rates users on a continuum that goes from denial to polarization to minimization to acceptance to adaptation.

We won't spend time going over each one of these, but let's briefly look at one: minimization. This is the most common category that takers fall in. People who fall into minimization recognize cultural differences but do not fully attend to those differences; instead, they highlight and value commonalties. There is much value in honing in on commonalities; in fact, it's usually one the more efficient ways to begin conversations with people we don't know. But deeper than what we have in common is what makes us different. The more we are able to recognize and respond appropriately to differences, the more culturally effective we are. If we can learn to bond over both our commonalities *and* our differences, we can gain a lot of ground in learning to love each other more completely. Jesus was always engaging those who were different from him. He did so by bringing a message of hope, justice, forgiveness, and salvation.

And lastly, the Cultural Intelligence Center (Cultural Q), has research-based assessments that measure individual orientations on ten cultural value dimensions (Cultural Values Profile) and measures capability for working and relating across cultures (CQ Assessment). This is slightly different from IDI because it is more focused on culture-specific rather than culture-general dimensions, although these can certainly overlap in some areas.

In the Cultural Values Profile, ten cultural dimensions are examined that play an important role in understanding how we relate to other cultures and how to better understand these dimensions as they represent other cultures. This doesn't just include ethnic groups from Southeast Asia or tribes in Sub-Saharan Africa, but can also be applied to the different cultures we encounter domestically every day. Let's briefly look at the dimensions here.

Individualism/Collectivism

Individualism: Emphasis on individual goals and individual rights

Collectivism: Emphasis on group goals and personal relationships

Context

Low Context (Direct): Emphasis on explicit communication (words)

High Context (Indirect): Emphasis on indirect communication (tone, context)

Power Distance

Low Power Distance: Emphasis on equality and shared decision-making

High Power Distance: Emphasis on differences in status; superiors make decisions

Being/Doing

Being: Emphasis on quality of life

Doing: Emphasis on being busy and meeting goals

Uncertainty Avoidance

Low Uncertainty Avoidance: Emphasis on flexibility and adaptability

High Uncertainty Avoidance: Emphasis on planning and predictability

Universalism/Particularism

Universalism: Emphasis on established rules and standards that apply to everyone

Particularism: Emphasis on unique standards based on specific relationships

Cooperative/Competitive

Cooperative: Emphasis on collaboration and a nurturing approach

Competitive: Emphasis on competition, assertiveness, and achievement

Expressiveness

Non-Expressive (Neutral): Emphasis on non-emotional communication and hiding feelings

Expressive (Affective): Emphasis on expressive communication and sharing feelings

Time Orientation

Short-Term Time Orientation: Emphasis on immediate outcomes (success now)

Long-Term Time Orientation: Emphasis on long term planning (success later)

Focus

Monochronic (Linear): Emphasis on one thing at a time; keep work and personal life separate

Polychronic (Non-Linear): Emphasis on different things at the same time; mix work and personal life

These dimensions are not always black and white; rather, they can be viewed more like a spectrum. Use this list as a resource when preparing to engage with different cultures or outgroup members. Understanding these dimensions can greatly help us understand people better, and to better identify a specific feature of why a person thinks or acts the way he or she does.

For example, I have a friend named Benjamin who is originally from Bhutan (of Nepalese, Tibetan, and Drukpa descent) but who moved to the US when he was nineteen. He is still able to remember very well and relate to the culture in which he used to live in Bhutan. His parents, who lived in the region most of their lives, still carry a large part of their culture with them, even though they live in a different place now.

Benjamin got married recently, and after his wedding he and his wife Leela didn't move into a place of their own; they continued to live with his parents. Now, for an American born-and-raised couple, continuing to live in one's parents' house would seem out of the question. We might easily think, "How can we have a life of our own if our parents are always around?" or "If we live with our parents, our individual choices may be compromised."

At first thought, American born-and-raised couples would likely think this is a *weird* practice. However, for Benjamin and Leela, the practice of *not* living with parents could be perceived as more culturally taboo to some in their community. In other words, it is not necessary to view Benjamin and Leela as living *with* his parents; rather, they all just live *together.* They share the bills, share the cooking and cleaning, and share their lives together. This is an example of a *collective* cultural practice, whereas an American born-and-raised couple who would insist on living by themselves represents a more *individual* cultural mindset. Neither practice is wrong or right. Benjamin's family, along with those of many other cultures, place a value on family that is not stronger or better than what born-and-raised Americans do, but one that is uniquely different than ours.

Understanding and responding appropriately to cultural differences helps us in cases like this. We don't always have to know the specific cultural dimensions that are in play, such as collectivism and individualism, although this knowledge is very helpful. What is important is developing the capacity to recognize when something is cultural. Instead of comparing them to our own culture, we can recognize the unique difference in the way their culture does things.

Cultural Misunderstandings

An Asian man lands an interview with a medium-sized US engineering company. He is familiar with some US culture, though he has received this information solely through media and through the English courses he has taken since he was young. He prepares himself for the interview by reading up on the company and going over practice questions that may be asked about his skills and experience.

He shows up for the interview fifteen minutes early and is dressed in a basic black suit and tie, appropriate for this type of interview even in his own culture. He informs the front desk associate, who is expecting him, and is escorted to a conference room where he waits for the manager and other senior team members for the interview. He is nervous, as any job candidate would be about this time, but he is also confident in his experience and abilities, and this interview is just another step in the process toward getting the job he wants and knows he is qualified for.

The door to the conference room opens; a man enters and introduces himself as the manager. The Asian man stands to greet and shake hands with the manager. However, the manager, who has been in the industry for a few decades and is a generation older than the Asian man, notices one thing in his greeting: he didn't make eye contact with him.

The manager blows it off at first and goes on with the interview, but a few questions in the manager starts to get annoyed by the Asian man's lack of eye contact. He stands up and declares the interview over. The Asian man is extremely confused about what is going on. The manager explains that he is being disrespectful and unprofessional because he has not looked him in the eye. The manager and the other senior team members exit the conference room.

One of the other team members, who has traveled to East Asia in the past and is somewhat familiar with the culture, stops the manager. She tries to explain that the reason the man is not making eye contact is because in his culture it is seen as more of a disrespectful gesture to those in authority positions. The manager pushes back and blows it off as a respect issue and not a cultural issue.

Although this is probably a more drastic example of a cultural misunderstanding, smaller-scale misunderstandings occur frequently when we are interacting with people from different cultures—and they occur not just with cultures from different parts of the world but with outgroups in our own neighborhoods.

Cultural Relativism

Culture is relative to context. Our practices and ways of life are relative to the context we are in, and this is just as true for other cultures. Remember to keep in mind the micro and macro levels of culture.

It is easy to compare the difference of cultures and to view why those differences are not like one's own culture instead, rather than ask why one's own culture might be the one that is different. When this happens, it's easy to label those cultures that do things differently as wrong or weird. But that same culture we might view as wrong or weird probably thinks the exact same thing about our culture. We might think it's weird that some cultures greet each other with a kiss on the cheek, because that is unusually intimate for someone we just met; but at the same time they might think it is weird that in the US we only greet each other with a handshake, a seemingly impersonal gesture. Or, "southerners" might think it's weird that "northerners" don't drink sweet tea while they think it's strange and distasteful to put sugar in iced tea.

The lesson here is that just because there is a feature of a culture that we are not used to or don't understand, it does not necessarily mean that it is wrong or weird. Practices and beliefs of cultures are best understood in their context; this is known as cultural relativism.

The good news here is that even if we struggle to recognize cultural differences through the context of others, we can know and trust that the good news of Jesus is relative to all cultures in all contexts. As we work toward understanding people in their cultures, let our motivation be the truth of Jesus, so that we can know how to communicate his message appropriately across all people and contexts.

Why Does Cultural Competence Matter?

Many scholars and anthropologists like to describe culture like an iceberg. We tend to only see the tip, but below and deep down there is a much greater presence. And oftentimes, when we see the "tip" of culture, we tend to point out the negative aspects of that culture. We need to dig deeper and try to understand the underlying constructs and influences of all outgroup members.

Cultural competence helps us navigate our surroundings and relationships in whatever context we may be in. Everything we do as human beings is relational. We have relationships in our jobs, universities, leisure activities, ministry activities, family, and more. Depending on the context, those relationships might look different in different compartments of our lives. When we think of family, we think of those who are closest to us: our spouses, children, parents, in-laws, and extended families. Our work or school relationships may be secondary, but they also take up quite a bit of our time and require some relational investment.

Cultural competence matters because it helps us navigate and understand our relationships, especially those relationships with people different from us. Cultural competence also matters because the world is growing closer and we are encountering more diversity than we ever have before. It is a unique opportunity, but one that must be carefully assessed and approached. Additionally, cultural competence is important because it helps us carry out the mission of God through loving, serving, and sharing with all types of people. When we better understand people and the culture they are a part of, we know how to love them better, serve them better, and communicate with them better.

Globalization

Globalization simply means that the world and its people are becoming closer and more accessible through advancements in technology—by means of transportation, communication, and digital and social media. As the world globalizes, we encounter more and more people from different cultures, and we are exposed to belief systems, norms, and worldviews that we are not used to. Sometimes these systems can make us uncomfortable because they seem so foreign. Children are encountering international students in their schools and neighborhoods; university students are sharing classes with international students and scholars; employers are hiring exchange visitors and international workers, as well as sending their employees to other countries to help them better compete in the global market. The global transportation industry is advancing through developments in faster airplanes, new and renovated airports, and more. We are able to travel with such ease now. Also, like never before, we are able to send communications to almost all parts of the world in an instant. We are also exposed to communications and media now more than ever.

Globalization is a broad theme of why cultural competence matters, but there are several other reasons as well. For Christians, becoming culturally competent means being able to effectively communicate and minister to those who represent a different culture than us. How are we to communicate and minister to the immigrant, the international student, or the minority neighborhood down the road from our own home if we don't have an understanding of how to interpret their world not through our eyes, but by learning to see it through theirs? A globalizing world means more opportunity to embrace people from all of the world with the love of Jesus.

Improving Cultural Competence

It's more difficult to recognize cultural differences until we are placed into a multicultural setting. Many of us go through life and don't think twice about cultural differences, while others may be always curious and eager for the chance to engage other cultures. As we work our way toward understanding contact, why it's important and needed, we should recognize that contact is a prime way to develop cultural competence.

There are a variety of ways to improve our cultural competence. We can read different books, watch movies, listen to music, keep journals of our cross-cultural encounters, be coached or mentored, attend cultural events and festivities, and more. Another way to improve cultural competence—and, I would argue, one of the more effective ways—is through contact.

Part of having success in contact is being able to gain perspective through truly realizing where the other person is coming from. People find success in this in different ways. Perhaps one of the most effective ways is by becoming a foreigner yourself. Often when people travel or live in different countries and begin trying to assimilate into a different culture, it's very challenging and difficult—because, well, being a foreigner is difficult. As you begin to learn about the culture and why they do things the way they do, your perspectives change, often affecting many of your prior beliefs and overall worldview. Jessica Udall wrote about how her experiences as a foreigner in Ethiopia grew her ability to love and welcome others in her book *Loving the Stranger*. She described how *becoming* a foreigner helped shape the way she was able to love immigrants, and she provides practical ways others can learn to love and serve foreigners.

I met Jessica at a conference in late 2017. We were in a focus group together and began chatting about what we were currently doing when she mentioned that she had written a book about cross-cultural engagement with immigrants. I focused in as we continued to discuss this, and briefly mentioned to her that I had been gathering notes for several months for my own potential book idea. I hadn't discussed my idea with very many people, because at the time I was very hesitant to write a book for a variety of reasons. As I explained this to Jessica and the thesis of my idea, I had never felt so encouraged by someone to begin this project. I'm thankful for my encounter with Jessica that day and I'm thankful for her "stranger experience."

We can all learn from having our own "stranger experiences." These experiences let us feel things we have never felt, see things we have never seen, and help us understand empathy on a whole new level. As we'll examine in the next chapter, several biblical characters had powerful "stranger experience" testimonies. So as we strive to continue to understand and adapt to the culture around us, let us do so with a yearning for listening and learning and understanding the importance of being culturally competent. Let us also do so by maintaining the historic salvific message of hope and justice that Jesus brings. Our ways of engaging culture and presenting the message of Jesus may need to be dynamic at times, but the message of Jesus itself always remains static.

Discussion

1. Self-reflect on your culture. How would you describe the culture you're a part of?

2. Would you consider yourself culturally competent? Why or why not?

3. How do you think understanding culture fits in with the gospel?

4. Looking back, can you think of a situation where you had a cultural misunderstanding but didn't realize it at the time? How did you respond at the time, and how would you respond differently now?

5. What are some examples in the Bible of people understanding and responding appropriately to cultural differences?

6. Have you ever had a "stranger experience?" How did you feel and what did you learn from it?

CHAPTER 7

THE BIBLE AND CONTACT

The Bible chronicles dramatically divine stories that can help us understand who God is more completely. In the process, we can relate to different characters of the Bible in different ways. Many of them had supernatural contact experiences with God, while others just had contact experiences with other people who led them closer in their contact with God.

When we study the contact moments of different characters and groups in the Bible, we learn that many of them wrestled with similar challenges that we still face today. As we study the following people and groups, let's imagine how their contact with God and with each other had an impact on the overarching story of redemption, and how each person or group was able to mature from the encounters they had and use those encounters to further the kingdom through relational love for one another.

Saul's Conversion

Paul had a supernatural contact experience with Jesus on the road to Damascus. Paul's life history is one of power and testimony to the power of encounter with Jesus. In Philippians 3, Paul gives a brief biography of his life before his contact moment with Jesus. He essentially describes himself as the "Jew of all Jews," and a persecutor of Christians. He grew up learning the law and was on his way up the Jewish ruling authority hierarchy. As news of Jesus began to spread, as recorded in the book of Acts, Paul took on the role of law-abiding justice warrior and persecuted and threatened Christians. It wasn't until Paul was on his way to Damascus to arrest followers of the Way that he heard the voice of Jesus:

> Meanwhile, Saul was still breathing out murderous threats against the Lord's disciples. He went to the high priest and asked him for letters to the synagogues in Damascus, so that if he found any there who belonged to the Way, whether men or women, he might take them as prisoners to Jerusalem. As he neared Damascus on his journey, suddenly a light from heaven flashed around him. He fell to the ground and heard a voice say to him, "Saul, Saul, why do you persecute me?"
>
> "Who are you, Lord?" Saul asked.
>
> "I am Jesus, whom you are persecuting," he replied. "Now get up and go into the city, and you will be told what you must do."
>
> The men traveling with Saul stood there speechless; they heard the sound but did not see anyone. Saul got up from the ground, but when he opened his eyes he could see nothing. So they led him by the hand into Damascus. For three days he was blind, and did not eat or drink anything.
>
> In Damascus there was a disciple named Ananias. The Lord called to him in a vision, "Ananias!"

"Yes, Lord," he answered.

The Lord told him, "Go to the house of Judas on Straight Street and ask for a man from Tarsus named Saul, for he is praying. In a vision he has seen a man named Ananias come and place his hands on him to restore his sight."

"Lord," Ananias answered, "I have heard many reports about this man and all the harm he has done to your holy people in Jerusalem. And he has come here with authority from the chief priests to arrest all who call on your name."

But the Lord said to Ananias, "Go! This man is my chosen instrument to proclaim my name to the Gentiles and their kings and to the people of Israel. I will show him how much he must suffer for my name."

Then Ananias went to the house and entered it. Placing his hands on Saul, he said, "Brother Saul, the Lord—Jesus, who appeared to you on the road as you were coming here—has sent me so that you may see again and be filled with the Holy Spirit." Immediately, something like scales fell from Saul's eyes, and he could see again. He got up and was baptized, and after taking some food, he regained his strength. (Acts 9:1–19)

For Paul, it took a supernatural encounter with Jesus for him to realize who Jesus was. Although Jesus might not usually speak to us in an audible voice as he did to Paul, we still have his words and example through the Bible. In this way, we must ask ourselves how we are like Paul and if our encounters with Jesus have resulted in scales falling from our eyes so we can see.

Furthermore, when we think about contact, there are several perspectives to this remarkable story. First, from Paul's perspective, he had an encounter with Jesus that resulted in an encounter with another man, Ananias. On one level, Paul's contact with Jesus was a supernatural experience that convicted him of his spiritual blindness, symbolically represented by his physical blindness during his encounter. His blindness and fasting were not necessarily punishment, but for a time of reflection due to the intensity of such an encounter with Jesus.[58] On another level, Paul's contact with Ananias was an event that helped Paul see, spiritually and physically. God chose to use contact encounters, first with himself to begin the process of making Paul "a chosen instrument" to carry his name, and then with Ananias as a vessel to continue that process.

Another perspective for viewing this comes from Ananias. When he had his vision of the Lord calling his name, Ananias responded with "Yes, Lord," similar to other responses Hebrew figures had to God when they were called upon (Abraham, Jacob, Moses, Samuel, Isaiah); Ananias was a devout observer of the law, as Paul later stated (Acts 22:12).

In this story, we may can find ourselves relating to Paul, not in the sense that we are persecuting Christians, but in the sense that we have some blindness in our life that only God can cure. He may give us a loud and clear sign like he did with Paul, or he may use a vessel like Ananias to come in contact with us to help us see better. Others of us might be able to relate to Ananias, hearing the call of God and saying, "Here I am!" God may be using us to encounter others who might need help seeing. Let's strive to have the same attitude of Ananias, being open and ready to respond to the call of God to encounter others, even if we perceive them as wrongdoers, like Ananias did with Paul. He clearly had questions about what was going on when the Lord called him, because he knew that Paul had been persecuting Christians. Nonetheless, God reaffirmed Ananias' calling, and he departed to go find Paul and answer God's call for him at that time.

Can we also relate to Ananias in the sense that even though we may seem open to the call of the Lord, there are people we may be skeptical of? In those situations, is our response, "Oh, you really don't mean *that* person/group, do you, Lord?" God reaffirmed to Ananias that he would make Paul an instrument for his glory; likewise, God continually reaffirms his call through the work Jesus has already carried out in his earthly ministry of setting the captives free (Luke 4:18) through the work he carried out on the cross, and through his resurrection and commission for us to go (Matt. 28:19). Let's work to not only keep saying, "Here I am, Lord!"—but, when we hear God calling us to contact with others, whether it's across the street or across the world, let our response and our actions be "yes."

Jew vs. Gentile

The "Jew and Greek" dynamic encompasses a broad theme in the New Testament, and especially captured in the book of Acts. There are many lessons to learn here about cultural diffusion and cultural differences. Understanding the overarching contact between Jews and Gentiles can give us valuable knowledge about what it means for vastly different cultural groups to unite over a common purpose. The contact moments that Jews and Greeks had serve as an inspiration to us, that we can also understand one another and see one another's perspective in light of our backgrounds and cultural differences.

To understand this, and before unwrapping the details, we first must understand the historical components in play. Christianity grew up in the external backdrop of Greco-Roman world. A monotheistic Jewish-originated religion spreading into a pluralist, philosophical society like Greece was bound to have profound implications for all involved. The area where Christianity was born and Jesus carried out his ministry, Palestine, was the product of Greek influence as well. Many of the Jews in Palestine had adopted Greek culture and values.

Before Jesus arrived on the scene, Alexander the Great had conquered much of the known world at the time. As a result, Greek influence spread throughout the regions and many of the people in those regions adopted the Greek language and social customs; this is known as Hellenism.[59] After Alexander died, the empire diffused and several of Alexander's successors ruled different regions. By about 300 BCE, Ptolemy I ruled Egypt and Seleucus ruled Syria, stretching from Asia Minor (Turkey) to Mesopotamia (Iraq).[60] Egypt, which was under control of Ptolemy, at the time included Palestine, the Jewish homeland.[61] However, around 200 BCE, the Ptolemaic dynasty was driven out of Palestine and the Seleucid dynasty assumed control of the region.[62] Antiochus, who referred to himself as Epiphanes (which means "God Manifest"), attempted to unify the different ethnic and religious groups in the region by forcefully promoting Hellenization.[63] Many Jews embraced the Greek ideas and social customs, while many resisted. Antiochus attempted to eradicate the Jewish faith as a whole by outlawing its practices, executing those who resisted, and even defaming the Jerusalem temple by erecting a statue of Zeus.[64]

There were, however, some Jews who were willing to die for what they believed in, known as the Hasidim.[65] The Maccabean Revolt eventually took place, in which a group of Jews were able to fight off the Syrian army and take back the temple in 164 BCE; this event today is known and celebrated as Hanukkah.[66] The Maccabees became kings, and a few years later a fatal decision to include Rome in their military affairs led to a decline in power. Eventually, Palestine became just another insignificant province in Rome.

Roman occupation in Palestine initiated a series of provincial governors, who are well-chronicled in the New Testament. The family of Herod ruled Palestine on behalf of the Roman Empire during the time of Jesus and were instrumental in his story. Herod the Great killed those who threatened his throne, including his wife and two sons, also providing the background for why he would order the murders of Bethlehem's children when he heard about the birth of King Jesus.[67]

The Roman Empire under Augustus (grandnephew of Julius Caesar) was even larger than Alexander's empire.[68] The vast empire included the rule of Judea, meaning that the dispersed Jews were living among Greeks, resulting in a lot of ethnic tensions which carried over well into the life of Jesus and after his death.

When Christianity began to spread, many Jews who had observed the law faithfully still kept many of their practices even as they followed Jesus, although Jesus had instituted a new covenant that didn't require the same standards of the old one. Paul addresses this in the book of Galatians, when he opposes Peter who seemed to be only eating with Jewish Christians; since many Jews and Gentiles ate separately because they still wanted to follow the Jewish dietary laws, Paul was worried that Peter was sending the wrong message to the Gentile Christians, making them feel left out or like second-class citizens in the church, and that this could threaten their understanding of justification by faith alone. Paul's rebuke of Peter was part of a longer address to the Galatians about how Christ's death brought a new covenant in this age, in which believers do not have to become Jews first or follow Jewish laws. Paul highlights this theme by saying, "There is neither Jew nor Gentile, neither slave nor free, nor is there male and female, for you are all one in Christ Jesus" (Gal. 3:28).

The application of this message still permeates us today as we continue to wrestle with inclusion, but Paul is saying that when we follow Jesus we have been crucified with him, and that it is no longer we who live, but Christ who lives in us (Gal. 2:20).

After Jesus resurrected and before he ascended, he gave his disciples a missional command: "you will be my witnesses in Jerusalem and in all Judea and Samaria, and to the end of the earth" (Acts 1:8). In this Jesus declares long before what Paul said about the gospel: it is for everyone—not just the Jews, but the outcast, the elite, and the whole earth.

Contacting the Outcast

Luke 9:51–56 chronicles an interesting event involving two of Jesus' disciples, James and John, and a village of Samaritans:

> As the time approached for him to be taken up to heaven, Jesus resolutely set out for Jerusalem. And he sent messengers on ahead, who went into a Samaritan village to get things ready for him; but the people there did not welcome him, because he was heading for Jerusalem. When the disciples James and John saw this, they asked, "Lord, do you want us to call fire down from heaven to destroy them?" But Jesus turned and rebuked them. Then he and his disciples went to another village.

An important note here is that this is the first mention in the book of Luke of Jesus' journey to Jerusalem, where he would resolve to fulfill the mission of God by dying on a cross. Part of the journey to Jerusalem involved going through Samaria. In this passage of Scripture, James and John were likely already wary of the Samaritans even before they arrived at the village. The journey from Galilee to Judea, where Jerusalem was, involved going through Samaria for the most expedient route. In a previous journey that Jesus had taken with his disciples from Judea back to Galilee, Scripture states that "he had to

go" through Samaria (John 4:4). This introduces the account of Jesus
and the Samaritan woman at the well. As it says that Jesus "had to
go," this could indicate that it was because Samaria was the shortest
route back to Galilee, or it could indicate that Jesus' sovereign plan
was to pass through Samaria as a necessity—not just as part of his
travel itinerary, but as part of his providential itinerary to demon-
strate the inclusion of the other into the new kingdom.[69]

Passing through Samaria when journeying between Judea and
Galilee was the usual route taken by travelers; however, strict Jews
would often bypass Samaria by taking a longer route that involved
crossing the Jordan River and going up or down the east side, to
avoid the risk of becoming "unclean" or "defiled."[70] Samaritans were
a racially mixed group of partly Jewish and partly Gentile ancestry,
and disdained and excluded by both Jews and non-Jews.

James and John had grown up in the Jewish culture that was
skeptical at best or hostile at worst to Samaritans. So when they
passed through the Samaritan village, their responses were indica-
tive of deeply rooted prejudices they had toward the Samaritans. To
earn the rebuke of Jesus in this instance seems like an intentional
wake-up call to James and John about how they viewed others who
were not necessarily like them. It also seems that Jesus could have
intentionally, knowing this situation would happen, brought James
and John to this moment as a way to facilitate an understanding that
those who are different don't deserve our ill will or punishment. Even
when they are not welcoming to us, as in this case, they deserve our
welcome and love, regardless of any reciprocity.

After Jesus' death, resurrection, and ascension, his disciples began
the task of taking the gospel to the ends of the earth. Throughout the
book of Acts, James and John worked to carry out the plan Jesus had
laid out for them. Interestingly, John finds himself back in Samaria,
this time with Peter.

> When the apostles in Jerusalem heard that Samaria had accepted the word of God, they sent Peter and John to Samaria. When they arrived, they prayed for the new believers there that they might receive the Holy Spirit, because the Holy Spirit had not yet come on any of them; they had simply been baptized in the name of the Lord Jesus. Then Peter and John placed their hands on them, and they received the Holy Spirit. (Acts 8:14–17)

Clearly something had changed within John. He went from wanting to "call down fire from heaven" onto the Samaritans to praying for them to receive the gift of the Holy Spirit. Jesus' ministry and example, and the indwelling of his Spirit, had an effect on John that caused him to see past people he may have been taught to dislike.

This story of John's influence from Jesus that impacted his contact with Samaritans—as well as the other stories in this chapter—is one that we can all learn from. Jesus knew that after his earthly ministry was over, his disciples would have to spread the good news to not just the Jews but to everyone else. Jesus exemplified this in his ministry, by coming into contact with the culturally outcast. What are we doing to follow the example of Jesus?

Discussion

1. Have you ever experienced a dramatic moment when "scales fell from your eyes" and you could see things correctly for the first time? Or have scales been falling more slowly from your eyes and you've begun to see more over time?

2. Is the Jew/Gentile dynamic relatable to our cultural climate today? If so, how?

3. Just as some Jewish Christians thought that Gentile converts should have subscribed to traditional Jewish cultural customs, do we ever expect converts outside our own culture to take on our specific customs? What might this look like?

4. What groups of people in our society could be considered outcast? What are we doing to reach and include these groups?

CHAPTER 8

REIMAGINING OUR APPROACH TO RELATIONSHIPS: PRACTICAL IDEAS AND CHALLENGES

Reimagining Our Friendships

The Barna Group released a report that involved a study on the state of friendships in the US. Their polling data confirmed that people tend to be drawn to those who are more like them. The poll asked adults if their friends were mostly similar or mostly different in areas such as religion, race or ethnicity, income, education level, social status, political views, and life stage. Of those people, the majority always leaned toward having friendships with others who were similar to themselves.[71]

Furthermore, the study revealed that evangelicals in particular are less likely than most to have friends who are different from them, especially when it comes to religious beliefs (91% mostly similar), ethnicity (88%), and political views (86%).[72]

These numbers can provide some insight and possible correlation as to why our society feels so polarized at times, and why many evangelicals feel cornered when it comes to navigating cultural challenges.

Area	Similar	Different
Religious Beliefs	62%	38%
Race or Ethnicity	74%	26%
Income	56%	44%
Education Level	63%	37%
Social Status	70%	30%
Political Views	62%	38%
Life Stage	69%	31%

Figure 1.   Results of Barna Group research, indicating areas of similarity and difference among friendships across the USA.

The percentages around race or ethnicity are especially striking. Evangelicals are often labeled as close-minded and unwilling to compromise by secular society and other religious groups. Sure, there are certain values of evangelicalism that can't be compromised, but the social stigma evangelicalism as a whole has received lately—including by some who don't want to be labeled as evangelical anymore because of the negative connotations associated with it—represents a possible flaw in how evangelicals have chosen to engage the world.

So why does it so often seem that evangelicals are at odds with many of the social and cultural debates lately? Is it because we have well thought-out, balanced, and informed perspectives of the situations and events? Sometimes yes; some people do put in the work it takes to understand where others are coming from. But much of the time it's because we haven't taken the chance of getting to know others who represent different sides of cultural issues. Spending intentional time with people who are of different religions, races, incomes, education levels, and political views can help us grow in the most positive and healthy ways. Again, we won't always end up agreeing with each other on every topic we discuss, and we shouldn't always end up agreeing with each other, but because of our personal interactions and seeing a different, respectful side of each other, we have a more complete view of each other that diminishes "otherness."

Our friendships with others can also affect how we generalize certain populations. In another report published by Barna, "In 2016, almost one-quarter (24 percent) of those who spent time with Muslim friends strongly disagreed that the majority of terrorism is perpetrated by Muslims. This is compared to 13 percent among those who did not spend time with Muslim friends."[73]

Given some of the statistics above, how can we not just improve the way we approach relationships with others but *reimagine* our view of others in a way that is consistent with God's view of us, because we were first imagined by him?

Most of us have neighbors who are a part of a different cultural or social group. They could be a different race, affiliated with a different political party, old enough to be our grandparents or young enough to be our grandchildren, struggling to get by financially, or refugees from the far side of the world. Nonetheless, we are all capable of sitting down for a meal and having a civil conversation to learn about each other. If we want a better world with substantive dialogue about our differences, we have to do the work to get there. One way to make this possible is to invite someone who is different from you to your home for a meal.

This chapter is geared toward providing a variety of practical ways in which we can reach out to others different from ourselves.

Many of us operate very busy and complex lives, and fitting in more relationships might seem daunting, but many of our existing casual relationships may already provide a key space of growing those into deeper more genuine relationships. I also recognize that not everyone's personality type may be conducive to all of these active approaches, I've tried to include a variety, but I hope those who may be more introverted can still engage those who share differences in communities they are already a part of, or use other imaginative ways to meet others.

Additionally, majority-culture people should take into account that creating contact with minorities should not be taken lightly. The truth is, some minorities may have had encounters with majority-culture people in the past that did not go well, or even induced some pain and trauma. As relationships begin to form, it's good to read the situation, and it may be good to communicate about this. The rest of the following brief sections provide some different areas of our lives to think about. They are not comprehensive sections, but will hopefully spark some new ideas about how to reimagine our approach to relationships.

Reimagining Our Church

Martin Luther King Jr. famously said that Sunday morning is the most segregated hour in America. There are numerous churches across the country who have made great strides in the step toward conciliation in their communities, but there must be a continual renewal among churches and individuals.

Another practical way to develop our cultural competency in pursuit of increasing our perspectives is to get to know or partner with local churches that are made up of a different demographic. Pastor Lee Jenkins (discussed earlier) started an initiative with another local church called the Conversations Moment, a movement formed out of the desire of Lee and the congregation he pastored and another local church pastor whose congregation was majority white. The two pastors got together and formed a plan for the members of the churches to "do life" with one another by spending time together, sharing meals together, and getting to know each other's stories. There are several avenues in which to approach racial issues within churches, but it seems that a good first step is getting members to come to the table together and promoting intentional conversation. I've talked to several people along the way in the journey of writing this, and I've heard so many times that it just takes some listening and not always interjecting.

Reimagining Our Engagement with the Foreigner

One incredible way to experience people from cultures outside of the US, and one close to my own heart, is to volunteer with a local organization that serves immigrants and refugees. There are currently nine volunteer agencies (VolAgs) designated by the US Department of State to resettle refugees, and there is usually at least one in each major metro area in the US. Refugees are some of the most vulnerable people in the world, and only a very few of them get resettled to a third country. Several VolAgs, six of which are religiously affiliated organizations, not only help with resettlement but also offer other services such as immigration legal services, employment services, English classes, and many more community-based services. They are always looking for volunteers to assist with the delivery of different services. During my time with World Relief, not only did volunteers help facilitate the duties of my job better, but the refugees enjoyed the company that came with other Americans spending time with them and investing in them as they learned to navigate US culture and customs.

Currently, about 13.7% of the total US population is foreign-born.[74] Immigrants of all categories, students, scholars, workers, and more represent an opportunity to be engaged. They all carry unique stories and culture with them.

Reimagining Our Consumer Approach

Many neighborhoods in our cities are composed of diverse groups of people, often largely separated from each other into clusters of their own city sections, a result of housing patterns that have been influenced for decades by some negative elements such as segregation, poverty, unethical mortgage lendings and home appraisals, but also other neutral elements such as cultural collectivity. In the areas of our cities that are racially or ethnically singular, there are usually shops, restaurants, markets, and other stores that are owned, managed, and frequented by the majority that lives in the area. This can also be an interesting cultural experience and a way to meet others from different cultural backgrounds.

By clueing into this, we step into the stranger identity and are able to better understand what life is like for minorities on a regular basis. By becoming the stranger, our discomfort and awkwardness can lead us to a greater empathy. Additionally, this is an excellent way to meet people who are different and probably don't live as far away as you might think. Martin Freeman, who costarred in the 2018 film *Black Panther*, was asked what it felt like as one of the few non-black actors on set, to which he responded, "You think, 'Right, this is what black actors feel like all the time?'"[75] Let's think critically about how our consumer approach can offer valuable contact moments.

Reimagining Our Entertainment

Probably one of the easier practical options to engage in is through our entertainment choices. Since moving to Atlanta, I have seen countless cultural festivities take place. Attending events and festivals is a great way to try foods, see art, hear music, learn history, and meet a variety of people. Now, obviously not everyone has the geographical advantage of living in a place that allows for such events on a regular basis, but when we reimagine our entertainment choices we must also consider movies, TV shows, books, music, and more. We can selectively choose movies that are a clear take on a cultural event, TV shows that have a cast culturally different from yourself, books written by minority authors, or music that presents varying perspectives and messages than what you are used to. By actively thinking about our entertainment choices, and engaging entertainment in a way that we can also learn more about others, we grow in our cultural competence.

Reimagining Our Mission

An incredibly fruitful and humbling way to come into contact with others is by participating in local and foreign missions. We first participate in mission because God has commanded us to: "Therefore go and make disciples of all nations, baptizing them in the name of the Father and of the Son and of the Holy Spirit, and teaching them to obey everything I have commanded you" (Matt. 28:19–20). We participate in mission by making disciples, and by proclaiming liberty to the captives and the oppressed and by healing the sick (Luke 4:18–19). The example of Jesus is clearly set for us in doing the same.

The product of participating in mission is that it usually involves coming into contact with others who represent a variety of different backgrounds that are likely different than your own. Just as Jesus intentionally came into contact with a variety of people, he exemplified a countercultural servant who loved all people. When we participate in mission, whether short-term or long-term, local or foreign, we garner an understanding of different people from different cultural backgrounds, whether they are from a different neighborhood in our own city or in a different country on the other side of the world.

By participating in mission, we recognize that not everyone had the same opportunities to excel in life, how spiritually deprived the world can be, and how in many cases not everyone even has the opportunity to live healthy physical and mental lives. Much of our foreign missions outreach to third-world environments consists of helping communities with shelter, nutrition, and other basic living standards we access so easily here. We visit these countries, see these poverty-stricken people, and our eyes are opened to the amount of suffering in the world. The challenge here is translating that recognition of suffering into a genuine understanding. Because the world affects different people in different ways than what we are used to seeing, we must also understand that people see the world differently because of that. Recognizing the plight of many in the world who live on less than we could ever imagine should give us a deeper understanding of humanity; in turn, our empathy for all people will be strengthened.

Missions helps us not only gain a deeper perspective of people from different backgrounds, but also gain a deeper understanding of God and his power. God is a missional God who desires everyone to know him and his truth (1 Tim. 2:4). Because God is a missional God who desires people, as followers of God we should desire the same. Let us pray that we can live missional lives without always being on "mission trips"; and let us pray that we can know people more, see them through the lens of God more fully, and know God more completely.

Reimagining Our Work

Many of us work in settings that already present us with opportunities to truly get to know people. Often our encounters at our jobs may seem personal because we spend a lot of time with coworkers, but they are more casual than they are genuine. Work is a tough place for a lot of people. It's one of the few places I can think of where we don't really get to choose the people we spend our time with. We are required to spend hours every day with people we may not really know. Some of us may work in places where we don't get along with our coworkers; in other cases, we are so different from them that investing time to get to know more about those differences seems tedious.

Yet others of us enjoy the people we work with and have good relationships with them. The next step, if it's not already in process, is to take those relationships to the next level, especially if they come from a different background or represent a different cultural group. In some cases, we may be hesitant to cross business and personal relations, but most US office settings and US culture in general allow for this, contrary to some cultures where this is more taboo and a different approach may need to be taken.

So what if we actively pursued learning from people instead of passively knowing about them? Think about it: Are we actively seeking real relationships with our coworkers who we spend so much time with already, or are we just casually encountering them, never learning about them, rarely taxing ourselves to see what their world is like?

Coworkers are the first category of people that I think of when I think of casual encounters. This is something that I have had to work on myself, and still am in many ways. Fortunately, I've always been blessed enough to work in fairly small offices that have allowed me to thoroughly get to know my coworkers for the most part. This is not the case for everyone.

Part of my reasoning for the *reimagining* label is because my thoughts and practices can only go so far when it comes to the specific settings each of us live in. By reimagining our relationships, we are challenged with thinking about how each of us, in the context God has placed us in, can engage people better. And if we can reimagine an approach to our relationships with our coworkers, perhaps we can learn and grow ourselves in the process.

Reimagining Our Proximity

There is power in being proximate to others. Michelle Warren writes about her experiences of moving into poor neighborhoods to be among the poor in her book *The Power of Proximity*. She discusses how becoming proximate to those who experience poverty is the best way for us to not only understand the plight of the poor but to also engage in carrying out justice for them. She says, "The most profound move you can make to address pain and injustice is to become proximate to it."[76]

I agree with Warren that proximity to the poor can be a transformational experience. I also believe that our proximity to anyone who comes from a different background or is from a different cultural group can be transformational if we display intentional contact with them. As highlighted earlier, research shows that proximity can change us and help us better understand the people we are around, but we must also continue to give credit to intentionality.

Warren's experiences of her and her husband moving into impoverished neighborhoods displayed an intentionality and a risk not many of us are willing to take. However, Warren was able to reimagine the way she engaged in carrying out justice for the poor by becoming physically close to them. By becoming intentionally proximate to others, we take a step toward knowing them, understanding them, and engaging in justice by helping, serving, and empowering them. Through this, we also develop our understanding of God and his world.

Have you ever considered becoming intentionally proximate to a group of people? Maybe it's moving to a poor neighborhood like

Warren, to a majority-Hispanic-occupied apartment complex, or to a different country altogether. There are a number of ways in which we can intentionally become proximate to others different than ourselves. Let's reimagine this part of our lives.

Part of what makes the redemptive contact of Jesus powerful and true is that he became proximate to humans by taking on the form of a man and physically coming to earth to engage humanity in redemptive action. Jesus serves as the best example of why we should also become proximate to others for the sake of redemptive contact.

Reimagining Our News

Probably the most controversial challenge listed here is the challenge of reimagining the way we engage our news and the media. It is a contentious subject in US culture for sure, and most people probably agree that the integrity of our current news and media ecosystems are at high risk if not already past any threshold of integrity standards. We've already looked at how the news and media can affect our relationships, but how can we educate ourselves to learn about current events without the filters that many news sources place on the information?

Perhaps one way to combat the current symptoms of media fragility is by examining sources on all sides of the spectrum, even the ones we may usually consider biased. As stated earlier, yes, some news sources *possibly* do exaggerate information and at worst completely distort it, but even within this, they could be including pieces of information about an event or story that you haven't recognized yet. As much as some of us may not want to watch certain news channels, or follow certain people on social media, sometimes they may be able to offer bits and pieces of information we didn't originally see or know about that can help us add to our own understanding of an event or story.

Sometimes trying to figure out the correct information about a subject is like putting together a puzzle. Some puzzles are easy and some hard, but we have to find the pieces and put them together. We have to put the work in, especially if they are subjects we want to discuss with others. It's kind of unfortunate, but the truth is, we all have to work harder to gain accurate news these days.

Reimagining Our Psychology

Psychology studies human behavior, including our social behavior and cognitive processes. Having awareness of how we functionally behave and respond to different situations can provide us insight into how we relate to and think about others. Growing our awareness of certain features of human behavior and cognitive processes, such as empathy and negativity bias, can help us not only understand others better, but also understand ourselves better.

Empathy

There is a long line of scholarship surrounding the neuroscience behind empathy. Simply stated, empathy is the ability to understand and share feelings of others. Empathy has been shown to improve our interpersonal relationships.[77] It motivates us for cooperative behavior and facilitates better communication among us, as well as fosters compassion.[78] Furthermore, empathy helps us feel more closely connected with each other and reduces the distance between us and others.[79]

When we understand what empathy is and try to practice it in our lives, people who might have seemed further away from us, for whatever reason, feel a little bit closer. This is because when we are able to protract our empathy toward others, we see them differently, we feel their situations differently, and we understand their souls differently. Our compassion for people grows; and as Christians, our love for them is deepened.

When we see some of the widespread human suffering going on in the world today, it can be easy to feel disconnected from it because of its massiveness; but when we take the time to know what's going on at an individual level, our empathy increases because it seems a little more personal.

There is another psychological concept closely related to the field of empathy called "psychic numbing." When the world is experiencing large-scale human suffering, our empathy for the masses may actually *decrease*—even though there is a higher quantity of people being affected—and actually develop more into apathy. But, when we can better grasp the story of an individual, our empathy is more likely to increase.

In September of 2015, a photo began circulating the internet of a three-year-old Syrian boy named Alan Kurdi. Alan had drowned in the Mediterranean Sea after the inflatable boat he was on capsized shortly after its departure from Turkey toward Greece; many might remember the image of his small body lying prone on the beach. In one study, psychologists analyzed the widespread reaction to the nature of the photograph. Google search trends revealed that search terms such as "Alan," "Syria," and "refugees" rose significantly in the following months.[80] They also tracked Swedish Red Cross donations that were specifically for a Syrian refugee campaign and found that they also increased significantly in the following weeks.[81] After the photo circulation began to decrease, searches and donations also decreased, despite the still incredibly high number of people suffering and fleeing their homes during this time. The photo of Alan did what statistics couldn't do. It grabbed their attention and helped many people act on their feelings about the photo.

What we can learn from a study like this is that the way we relate to individuals can also impact the way we relate to the many. It probably shouldn't take an individual experience to grab our attention and catalyze our action toward the larger group, but sometimes that is what it takes.

In our contact with individuals, let's also be wary of how that contact controls our thoughts of entire groups. Not all individuals are representative of the group they may be a part of, and not all groups are representative of all the individuals they consist of. Let's not grow numb or let our compassion fade at the plight of the masses, but let's empathize with them just as we hurt with the individuals. Let's allow our contact with individuals also help us understand the group.

Negativity Bias

More often than not, when we have limited interactions and relationships with those who are different from us, our psychological processes tend to associate negativity with them or their group as a whole. Even in situations where we are exposed to equally positive, neutral, and negative traits of certain people or groups, we tend to highlight the negative traits more than the positive ones. In psychology, this is known as *negativity bias*, because we are biased toward pronouncing the negative attributes of people or groups that we don't know well or are different from us. So even when people display attitudes or actions we consider positive, those thoughts and actions are likely hidden by our biases to highlight any negative features, even if they are minuscule.

Do you know someone who you feel like goes out of their way to find something wrong with everything? Or someone who never gives the benefit of doubt to others? We all show signs of doing these things, but some people may have a propensity to show more negative bias than others. After the tragedy of the Dallas police shooting in 2016, former President George W. Bush speaking at the memorial service said, "Too often, we judge other groups by their worst examples, while judging ourselves by our best intentions. . . . And this has strained our bonds of understanding and common purpose."[82] This couldn't be more true and representative of negativity bias, especially given many of the cultural events occurring around the country and the world where we see blame being placed on whole groups for the actions of a few individuals. We gravitate toward the negative characters of the group more than we ever even recognize the positive contributions of said group.

We have all probably felt the effects of people categorizing us as well. Here is a light example: I'm a big fan of LeBron James; I have been following him since about 2003. Often when I'm having a discussion about basketball or the NBA with someone and they ask me who my favorite player is and I tell them LeBron, they'll kind of smirk or roll their eyes as if it's cliché or too easy to be a fan of LeBron. It's easy for them to categorize me as a bandwagon fan, which has a negative perception—and I *am* a bandwagon fan in the sense that I root for LeBron no matter what team he is playing for. But upon explaining my reasoning for being a fan of his, it makes more sense. First, I've been a fan of his since I was young, before he made his title runs, before he won multiple MVPs, before he was in the GOAT (greatest of all time) conversation. Not to mention his exceptional charity off the court. I'm not going to change who my favorite player is just because he became the best player in the league and one of the most popular athletes in the world, for the sake of not being cliché. Sometimes we just need to give people a chance to explain themselves before we make quick categorizations.

We all have tendencies to associate negative or perceived negative traits of groups with individuals. Certainly we have all seen examples like this, and sometimes they are true, but it's our negativity bias that makes them more pronounced and it more likely for us to associate entire groups of people with what we might perceive as negative, thus oversimplifying and stereotyping them. Negative voices and actions tend to speak the loudest, so we must be aware of this and actively seek to negate any unfounded biases we have toward individuals or groups.

Likewise, we generalize entire groups of people based off the negative actions of just a few individuals. We can consider recent examples of some tragic events such as an undocumented immigrant murdering a citizen, a white man shooting up a place of worship, a white police officer killing an unarmed black man, or a young black teen committing a crime. The reality is, depending on our preconceived biases toward the events, we can easily generalize all immigrants as hardened criminals, all white men with guns as terrorists, or all black teenagers as troublemakers.

We can remedy this by coming into contact with a variety of people from any of these groups and others. Coming into contact with them helps us to understand them and helps us defeat the negative biases we may have toward them. By truly getting to know people who are members of groups we may easily generalize, our categorizations of them decrease. By getting to know them, we can more easily focus on the positive traits of them instead of the small negative ones we may usually think of. We have to gear ourselves toward showing people more grace, not expecting everyone different from us to be perfect, and giving more people the benefit of the doubt—because Jesus has also shown us unlimited grace, knows that we will still make mistakes, and has already given us the benefit of the doubt by dying on the cross for our sins.

What If?

What if we were able to put some of these practical examples and challenges into practice? You aren't expected to start practicing each of these immediately, but perhaps some of these you could begin today or tomorrow. How would your life look if you understood empathy well and were able to practice it, with both the individuals and the masses? How would your job look if you actively considered intentional relationships with your coworkers who are different from you? What if you bought your groceries in the predominantly Hispanic neighborhood store not far from your own neighborhood? How could your family benefit from attending an international food festival one weekend? What could you learn from the next book you read if it's written by an author of a different race or background? All of these are just a few ways we can reimagine our lives and approach relationships in our lives with people different than us.

This is how we reimagine our approach to relationships: by intentionally bonding with people who we share differences or even disagreements with. We spend time with others who didn't grow up like we did or who may have not had the same opportunities as us, and get to know how their upbringing influenced who they are today. So let's spend time practicing some of these things.

The Redemptive Process in Action

As we process what it means to engage others through intentional contact, and reimagine our approach to relationships through understanding, let us also consider the redemptive impact it has. Sometimes we are hesitant or just downright resistant to build relationships with others. Whatever hostilities we have toward others and whatever they are rooted in, we must confront those and address the reasons behind those hostilities, because God has also received us despite our hostilities. "God's reception of hostile humanity into divine communion is a model of how human beings should relate to the other."[83] By this, we are able to capture, through our relationships with others, a picture of God's redemptive process.

In the redemptive process, those who believe in God are brought in by Him who forgets and forgives their past and guides them into the future. The way we receive, engage, and respond to others should be likened to the way that God has received, engaged, and responded to us—by allowing Jesus to be the redemptive point of contact to whom we all are invited. Let's receive others with open hearts. Let's engage others with intentionality. Let's respond to others appropriately, just as he has done all of this for us.

Discussion

1. How would you describe your friend groups? Do you have friends who are different, in any of the dimensions listed in Figure 1? If so, what have you learned from them?

2. Which of the "reimagining" areas stick out to you the most? How can you practically engage within each of those areas?

3. Which of these areas seem most challenging to engage in? Why?

4. When have you been on the receiving end of negativity bias? What about the giving end?

5. What other ways can you reimagine your approach to relationships that reflect the redemptive process in action?

CHAPTER 9

OPPORTUNITY IS WAITING

Bridging the Gap

When I grew up in Mississippi, I had no clue what it meant to value each other's differences. Although I had plenty of opportunity to be exposed to the unique cultures of others, I never really paid attention to them until I was older. Most people might think a place like Mississippi lacks diversity and cultural diffusion, and it does, compared to other states. According to the US Census Bureau, about 2.3% of Mississippi's population is foreign-born, compared to the national average of about 13.7%.[84] However, Mississippi is seeing growth in this area. In 2000, the foreign-born population was only about 1.4%.[85]

It's also important to note the two most populous demographic groups in Mississippi are blacks (37%) and whites (59%).[86] So although Mississippi is not as ethnically or internationally diverse as some other states, it is still has some racial diversity—and anywhere there is diversity, there are bound to be cultural differences we can learn about. And race isn't the only dimension of diversity where contact moments abound. Creating contact moments can also be applied with an intersectional approach, that is, within any areas of difference. We are currently living in one of the most opportune moments in history when it comes to loving our neighbors, so let's bridge the gap between relationships and seize the opportunities we have to love and learn from others different from ourselves.

Where Do We Draw the Line? Or Is There a Line?

I can imagine some people reading this thinking, "Should I really try to understand the perspective of people who share completely opposite views about some of my deepest convictions? Where is that going to lead? Where do I draw the line?" Certainly each of us are all going to carry deeply held convictions about certain topics, especially our faith. But the question here may actually be more along the lines of, "How do I listen well and understand without showing my acceptance if it's something I disagree with or have a deep conviction about?" How do we navigate getting to know and coming in contact with people who might hold views that may be in stark contrast of our convictions? Many times, for Christians, these convictions are rooted in Scripture.

How do we navigate the question of "Where do I draw the line?" First, I challenge you to challenge what you think you know. Some of you may have already been through seasons of life where you have done this or continually do so as a way to grow and learn. My plea to those who have not challenged what they think they know is to ask themselves where their knowledge and beliefs come from. For example, are these views liturgical and a product of your environmental upbringing in your family or church? This is often the case for many Christians who were raised in church and in Christian homes. However, there comes a point that we all need to go through a season of genuine questioning in order to either better develop those beliefs or in some cases just lose some of them— especially if they are more rooted in things you have only heard others say and not in actual biblical and theological research you have done yourself.

I remember going through a season in college where I was constantly asking questions about why I was raised the way I was, why I was raised in the church I grew up in, why my church believed this or that, etc. This questioning truly led me to a stronger and more vibrant faith in the Lord. I sought out perspectives of people who grew up differently than me, and I still strive to continue learning and challenge what I know because it makes my faith stronger. We don't challenge ourselves in this way necessarily to void our initial views or convictions, but to explore them in new ways with new perspectives so that they become more developed. And in some cases along the way, we make larger modifications to our entire worldviews.

There are many areas in which we can challenge ourselves—climate change, immigration, capital punishment, the roles of church and state, abortion, sexual ethics, civil obedience, and more. Each one has a different difficulty level for each of us. When we wrestle with our thoughts around these topics and so many others, one of the best ways to learn apart from biblical guidance is to learn how other people have learned to navigate these topics. In these cases we need to recognize that our goal in conversation is not to get the other person to always believe what you believe but to listen to them, respond gently to them about the way you have reasoned with such topics, learn from them, nuance or change your views when necessary, and make your faith stronger through it all.

With this in mind, we learn that it is acceptable to strive to understand our neighbors' views, no matter how far off they may be from ours, while still maintaining our most deeply held convictions around certain topics. We can and we should always listen, but listening and gaining perspective does not always equal sacrificing our convictions or showing acceptance. It does mean respecting those who don't share the same convictions, even if they are issues that are deep. If this is the case, we can't forget that we can also provide why we believe what we believe and why their views around some topics may be missing some pieces. But it is very important to be careful about using this simply to change someone's mind. If we go into conversations with the end result of mind-changing, most of the time we will fail.

And yes, when conversing with non-Christians (and perhaps even many who identify as Christian), we will perceive them to have blindness in some areas that aren't consistent with our Christian faith. But we continue to listen, we learn, and we gently and peacefully share how God has impacted our beliefs. And only God can change someone's mind or cure blindness. Alister McGrath says it like this: "Arguments do not cure blindness, nor does the accumulation of evidence, powerful rhetoric, or a compelling personal testimony. Blindness needs to be healed, and such a healing is something only God is able to do. God alone is able to open the eyes of the blind and enable them to see the realities of life."[87]

So where do we draw the line? Did Jesus draw lines when it came to who he would talk to and who he wouldn't? I think that Jesus didn't draw any lines in this area, for a few reasons. First, his command to love your neighbor as yourself broke all existing lines in the culture, also represented by Jesus' example in eating with and coming into contact with "sinners" and the "unclean." Secondly, perhaps Jesus never had a line because if he had given us one, we would always be as close as possible to that line without crossing it. If Jesus had drawn the line at conversing with and healing the sick and had an attitude of, "Don't get too close or you may get sick," his life and ministry would have looked completely different.

Jesus didn't just obliterate all lines when it came to contact with others, and he's not just telling us to erase the lines we may have created in our own lives, but he's telling us through his words and through his example to cross lines in countercultural ways. Jesus crossed all lines of conversation when it came to contact with others, and we are called to do the same. So the question may not be, "Where do I draw the line?" but "What lines can I cross?"

Embrace the Difference

Historically, we have let differences distract us from truly getting to know others. But what if we were able to embrace our differences? Instead of always saying things like, "We only concentrate on what we have in common," or "We don't talk about our differences because we know it won't end well," what if our way forward was to just learn how to make those conversations about difference end well? This is how we reimagine our approach to relationships: by getting to know one another and ending our conversations well.

As important as our differences are, let us not forget the reason why those differences are important. God made us different, but he has given us the opportunity to unite around a common name, the name of Jesus. It's easy to unite around the idea that people get to God through Jesus, but we must ponder the question of "Does everyone get to Jesus the same way?" Our paths to Jesus often look different, especially in different cultures. The way I came to know Jesus probably looks vastly different than a Chinese Christian's way of coming to know Jesus. Likewise, my way of coming to know Jesus probably looks much different than some of my black brothers' and sisters' ways of coming to Jesus.

It may seem like a paradox—uniting around what makes us different—but when we think about our path toward loving and embracing others who are different, if we are apathetic toward the difference—or worse, if we completely dismiss the difference—we set ourselves up for failure, because our apathy or dismissal is basically concluding that we expect everyone we pursue relationships with to accept our way of thinking and our way of doing things. It's tempting relate attention to difference as acquiescence, but it's not that at all. Attention to difference is simply understanding.

Seizing a Closer World

In a globalizing world, we have the opportunity to expose ourselves to various differences including backgrounds, opinions, beliefs, etc., while strengthening our own. Some people might fear a world that is globalizing and becoming more blended; but for Christians, a globalizing world that exposes us to various races, ethnicities, and nationalities essentially brings us an element of heaven on earth, as examined earlier.

But it doesn't take the world becoming closer together for us to learn about and come in contact with people different than us. As impactful as this phenomenon has been over recent decades and will continue to be, we have the opportunity to engage others who have been around us for years. We are always surrounded by opportunities to learn from people who are different. Even for the introvert, there are a variety of ways to know others well through some of the practical examples we looked at in the last chapter.

Some of us are genuinely intrigued by diversity and people from different cultures because diversity represents the creativity of God and how he is able to form so many different human beings physically and culturally, all made in his image. Others of us may be hesitant about diversity because it might come with the stigma of a political label trying to promote an agenda, and in some cases this may be true. However, if we are able to block out external factors that influence our ability to value diversity, we will also have more opportunity to value the views that come with diversity. Let's seize the opportunities that are around us, learn from others, and learn to love them well.

Opportunity to Welcome

The greatest example of authentic welcome was and is still Jesus. Jesus crossed lines in the first-century Jewish world that astonished people. The welcome he displayed to others teaches us that our own ideas of welcome should know no bounds.

> Now the tax collectors and sinners were all gathering around to hear Jesus. But the Pharisees and the teachers of the law muttered, "This man welcomes sinners and eats with them." (Luke 15:1–2)

Tax collectors and sinners were often referred to together in the gospel accounts. Tax collectors were not very well liked by others; they were looked at as corrupt, dishonest, and greedy, as well as unclean by pious Jews because of their contact with Gentiles. Jesus welcomed the social and the religious outcasts and ate with them. Such countercultural acts had additional implications at the time, because eating with "unclean" or defiled sinners meant risking becoming unclean or defiled as well. But Jesus, as the savior, came to make the unclean clean. Just as he could cleanse the leper (Luke 5:12–13) without being made unclean, he redeems the sinner without being defiled.

Jesus is the prime example to look to when it comes to contact with the other. Our hesitations to have intentional contact with those who are different—whether they are seen as unclean in our eyes because of their race, ethnicity, nationality, social standing, sexual orientation, income level, education level, political affiliation, religion, sin, etc.—should be thwarted by the example and action of Jesus. Whatever fears we may have when it comes to contacting and welcoming people, let's continually consider the example of Jesus and how to actively live out the way he not only welcomed outcasted and sinful humanity on an earthly level, but also how he welcomes us on a salvific level regardless of who we are, the mistakes we may have made, and all the other things that deserve to separate us from him. He welcomes us and accepts us anyway.

Opportunity to Love

As we have been examining, Jesus was (and is) the ultimate example of what love is and how to love well. The words of Jesus call us to love well, and we know that love should be the distinguishing mark of his followers: "A new command I give you: Love one another. As I have loved you, so you must love one another. By this everyone will know that you are my disciples, if you love one another" (John 13:34–35). The command to love others was not new even in Jesus' time, but here Jesus emphasizes that we are called to love others *just as Jesus has loved us.* The life and ministry of Jesus transformed the idea of loving others by crossing lines and spending time with people who otherwise wouldn't deserve it. Jesus even tells us to love our enemies (Matt. 5:44). Through it all, Jesus calls us to love distinguishably, to love uniquely, and to love all, including our enemies. Have you been challenged to love well lately? If you haven't, now is the opportunity to love others well through contact with them.

Opportunity to Share

The greatest opportunity that we have to share with others is by coming into contact with them. Our contact with others should be driven by love and by the desire to learn more about who they are. As Christians, we are also driven by the command of Jesus to make disciples—and what better avenue of doing so than coming into intentional contact with others?

Contact is an opportunity to share just as much as it is an opportunity to learn. However, our opportunity to share should strictly be rooted in love and not in any false piety that relays strict outcomes of proselytization. No, we follow Jesus and his example by coming in contact with others, sharing his love through service and freedom from oppression, as well as sharing his love through the telling of his love and the meaning of a life-altering relationship with him that results in the eternal. Through contact, let's show others the real contact that changes everything—a type of contact that triggers repentance and demands full devotion, but the type of contact that brings the most joy.

Frequently, though, we will find ourselves just trying to learn from people who are already Christians, in which our contact with them presents opportunities to learn and share in different ways. Let's share whatever we have to share with love, and let's seek opportunities to follow the example of Jesus.

Discussion

1. Do you struggle with your willingness to learn from people who hold different views or values because you're afraid of appearing as if you accept those views or values? Why do you think this is?

2. What lines did Jesus cross in his day that were considered countercultural?

3. After reading through the book, what is your understanding of globalization and how Christians can thrive within it?

4. What opportunities can you think of that offer you the chance to welcome, love, and share with others not like yourself?

CONCLUSION

Fall in Love with People

As we transition to the end, a very short and appropriate summary for this book could be described as a call to "fall in love with people." That's it. We fall in love with people by pursuing the life Jesus has set for us—not as mere bystanders who only see and comment on what's going on, but as active players who participate in knowing people created by God by actively welcoming, loving, serving, and sharing with them. Jesus calls us all who identify with him to fall in love with people by welcoming and eating with sinners; serving strangers, widows, orphans, and prisoners; and setting the captives free. We strive to come into intentional contact with others because it opens our minds, hearts, and hands to who people are, made in the image of God. This is modeling incarnation.

As we have examined in this book, our call to fall in love with people is rooted in who Jesus was. We love people because Jesus has loved us. We come in contact with people who we may not usually be in contact with because Jesus did so, and we recognize the redemptive contact that we have had with Jesus as a path to reconcile with God. In turn, we also view our contact with people as a redemptive way to foster community, conciliation among ourselves, learning, and being made whole as a people of God set out for his glory.

From Theory to Certainty

Examining contact theory has given us a scaffolding that uses evidence to help us understand and grow our ability to come in contact with others. Through this theory, we see how contact with others different from ourselves increases our understanding of them while reducing any prejudice we may have against them. We utilize the conditions of successful contact to help us have more efficient and effective relationship-based contact.

While God has given us the gift and ability to utilize research as a way to understand his creation more deeply, we grasp specific research much better when we understand that we are catching up to what the Bible already displays and what God already desires. In this sense, we move from theory to certainty because despite the successful evidence gathered throughout years of social-psychological research in this field, and although it gives us confidence that our intentional contact with others is effective in helping us grow and understand God's people better, it still isn't perfect. Perfection is only certain with God, and we can only be certain about the way we interact with and treat others when we base it and layer it with God. Theoretical research has its ups and downs, but with God there is always certainty. God is not a hypothesis, nor a theory, but a certainty that continually carries us through darkness and into light.

And we can be certain that when we put our faith in Jesus, believe in him, admit to where we have been wrong, and continue to grow in him, we have a new life and are seen in new light, and we are also able to see others in that new light. Because God has chosen us and sees us in this new light that is founded in his love for us, let us also always strive to see people the way God sees them, with love, potential, and light.

ENDNOTES

[1] "Roswell, Georgia," City-Data.com, accessed December 5, 2019, http://www.city-data.com/city/Roswell-Georgia.html.

[2] "prejudice (n.)," *Merriam-Webster*, accessed May 24, 2019, https://www.merriam-webster.com/dictionary/prejudice?utm_campaign=sd&utm_medium=serp&utm_source=jsonl.

Chapter 1

[3] Matthew Shaer, "Ellis Island South: Welcome to the Most Diverse Square Mile in America," Atlanta, January 19, 2017, https://www.atlantamagazine.com/great-reads/ellis-island-south-welcome-diverse-square-mile-america.

[4] US Census Bureau, "QuickFacts: Mississippi," Population Estimates, July 1, 2018 (V2018), accessed January 24, 2019, https://www.census.gov/quickfacts/ms.

Chapter 2

[5] "Plessy v. Ferguson," History.com, last modified August 21, 2018, https://www.history.com/topics/black-history/plessy-v-ferguson.

[6] Wade Henderson and Judith A. Brown, "Building Housing and Communities Fifty Years after 'Brown v. Board of Education.'" *Journal of Affordable Housing & Community Development Law* 13, no. 4 (Summer 2004): 437–42, https://www.jstor.org/stable/25782709?seq=1#page_scan_tab_contents.

[7] "Brown v. Board: Timeline of School Integration in the U.S," *Teaching Tolerance*, accessed February 8, 2019, https://www.tolerance.org/magazine/spring-2004/brown-v-board-timeline-of-school-integration-in-the-us.

[8] Thomas F. Pettigrew, et al., "Recent Advances in Intergroup Contact Theory," *International Journal of Intercultural Relations* 35, no. 3 (2011): 272.

[9] Thomas F. Pettigrew and Linda R. Tropp, "A Meta-Analytic Test of Intergroup Contact Theory." *Journal of Personality and Social Psychology* 90, no. 5 (2006): 751.

[10] Ibid., 751.

[11] Pettigrew, et al., "Recent Advances," 272.

[12] Ibid., 272.

[13] Pettigrew and Tropp, "Meta-Analytic," 751–752.

[14] Ibid., 752.

[15] Pettigrew, et al., "Recent Advances," 274.

[16] Thomas F. Pettigrew, "Intergroup Contact Theory." *Annual Review of Psychology* 49 (1998): 66.

[17] Ibid.

[18] Ibid., 67.

[19] Ibid.

[20] See Pettigrew and Tropp, "Meta-Analytic," 753; Pettigrew, et al., "Recent Advances," 275.

[21] Ibid., 276.

[22] Ibid.

[23] Ibid.

Chapter 3

[24] Pew Research Center, "The Partisan Divide on Political Values Grows Even Wider," October 5, 2017, accessed February 8, 2019, https://www.people-press.org/2017/10/05/the-partisan-divide-on-political-values-grows-even-wider.

[25] Ibid.

[26] Amy B. Wang, "'Post-truth' Named 2016 Word of the Year by Oxford Dictionaries," *Washington Post*, November 16, 2016, accessed February 8, 2019, https://www.washingtonpost.com/news/the-fix/wp/2016/11/16/post-truth-named-2016-word-of-the-year-by-oxford-dictionaries/?utm_term=.19617623944.

[27] "post-truth (adj.)," *Oxford Living Dictionaries*, accessed February 8, 2019, https://en.oxforddictionaries.com/definition/post-truth.

[28] Brendan Nyhan and Jason Reifler, "When Corrections Fail: The Persistence of Political Misperceptions," *Political Behavior* 32, no. 2 (June 2010): 303–30, https://www.jstor.org/stable/40587320.

[29] John Piper, "Why Do Christians Preach and Sing? Spectacular News and the Beauty of Christ," sermon/video, Passion Conference, Atlanta, January 3, 2015, https://vimeo.com/showcase/2105136/video/119993435.

[30] *ESV Study Bible* (Wheaton, IL: Crossway, 2008), 2019.

[31] Neff Associates, "The History of Public Relations," July 3, 2015, http://neffassociates.com/the-history-of-public-relations.

[32] Ibid.

[33] The Museum of Public Relations, "Public Relations through the Ages: A Timeline of Social Movements, Technology Milestones and the Rise of the Profession," accessed May 20, 2019, http://www.prmuseum.org/pr-timeline.

Chapter 4

[34] Miroslav Volf, *Exclusion and Embrace: A Theological Exploration of Identity, Otherness and Reconciliation* (Nashville: Abingdon Press, 1996), 85, Kindle edition.

[35] Ed Stetzer, *Christians in the Age of Outrage: How to Bring Our Best When the World Is at Its Worst* (Carol Stream, IL: Tyndale Momentum, 2018), xiii, Kindle edition.

[36] Brian M. Howell and Jenell W. Paris, *Introducing Cultural Anthropology: A Christian Perspective* (Grand Rapids, MI: Baker Academic, 2010), 44.

[37] Ibid.

Chapter 5

[38] James Lankford and Tim Scott, "Americans Should Dine with Families of Other Races," *Time*, July 28, 2016, http://time.com/4428490/america-race-relations.

[39] Ibid.

[40] Ibid.

[41] Ibid.

[42] Ibid.

[43] Elyse Wanshel, "Black Man Gets KKK Members to Disavow by Befriending Them," *Huffington Post*, December 22, 2016, https://www.huffingtonpost.com/entry/black-man-daryl-davis-befriends-kkk-documentary-accidental-courtesy_us_585c250de4b0de3a08f495fc.

[44] Conor Friedersdorf, "The Audacity of Talking about Race with the KKK," *Atlantic*, March 27, 2015, https://www.theatlantic.com/politics/archive/2015/03/the-audacity-of-talking-about-race-with-the-klu-klux-klan/388733.

[45] Ibid.

[46] Wanshel, "Black Man Gets KKK Members to Disavow."

[47] Jeffrey Fleishman, "A Black Man's Quixotic Quest to Quell the Racism of the KKK, One Robe at a Time," *Los Angeles Times*, December 8, 2016, http://www.latimes.com/entertainment/movies/la-ca-film-accidental-courtesy-20161205-story.html.

[48] Wanshel, "Black Man Gets KKK Members to Disavow."

[49] Austin Hamilton, in discussion with author, November 2018.

[50] Derek McClardy, in discussion with the author, November 2018.

Chapter 6

[51] "culture (n.)," *Merriam-Webster*, accessed May 24, 2019, https://www.merriam-webster.com/dictionary/culture.

[52] Ibid.

[53] Terry L. Cross, et al., "Towards a Culturally Competent System of Care: A Monograph on Effective Services for Minority Children Who Are Severely Emotionally Disturbed," March 1, 1989, 13, https://files.eric.ed.gov/fulltext/ED330171.pdf.

[54] "About Cultural Intelligence," Cultural Intelligence Center, accessed May 24, 2019, https://culturalq.com/what-is-cq/.

[55] "The Re-working of 'Work,'" IFTF, accessed May 24, 2019, http://www.iftf.org/futureworkskills.

[56] Bernard Marr, "The 10+ Most Important Job Skills Every Company Will Be Looking for in 2020," *Forbes*, October 28, 2019, accessed November 23, 2019, https://www.forbes.com/sites/bernardmarr/2019/10/28/the-10-most-important-job-skills-every-company-will-be-looking-for-in-2020/#15d9cd6467b6.

[57] David Livermore and Linn Van Dyne, "Cultural Intelligence: The Essential Intelligence for the 21st Century," Cultural Intelligence Center, accessed May 24, 2019, 8–10, https://culturalq.com/wp-content/uploads/2016/05/SHRM-report.pdf.

Chapter 7

[58] *ESV Study Bible*, 2099.

[59] Stephen L. Harris. *The New Testament: A Students Introduction*. (Boston: McGraw-Hill Higher Education, 2006), 45.

[60] Ibid., 64.

[61] Ibid.

[62] Ibid.

[63] Ibid.

[64] Ibid.

[65] Ibid.

[66] Ibid., 67.

[67] Ibid., 69.

[68] Ibid.

[69] *ESV Study Bible*, 2027.

[70] Ibid.

Chapter 8

[71] Barna Group, "U.S. Adults Have Few Friends—and They're Mostly Alike," October 23, 2018, https://www.barna.com/research/friends-loneliness.

[72] Ibid.

[73] Barna Group, "Americans Soften on Immigration in 2017," September 19, 2017, https://www.barna.com/research/americans-soften-immigration-2017.

[74] U.S. Census Bureau, "American FactFinder," accessed May 24, 2019, https://factfinder.census.gov/faces/tableservices/jsf/pages/productview.xhtml?pid=ACS_17_1YR_S0501&prodType=table.

[75] *"Black Panther:* Trivia," IMDb, accessed May 24, 2019, https://www.imdb.com/title/tt1825683/trivia?ref_=tt_trv_trv.

[76] Michelle F. Warren, *The Power of Proximity: Moving Beyond Awareness to Action* (Downers Grove, IL: IVP Books, 2017), 7, Kindle edition.

[77] Mark H. Davis, "Measuring Individual Differences in Empathy: Evidence for a Multidimensional Approach," *Journal of Personality and Social Psychology* 44, no. 1 (1983): 113–26.

[78] Frederique De Vignemont and Tania Singer, "The Empathic Brain: How, When and Why?" *Trends in Cognitive Sciences* 10, no. 10 (2006): 435.

[79] Vittorio Gallese, "Mirror Neurons, Embodied Simulation, and the Neural Basis of Social Identification," *Psychoanalytic Dialogues* 19, no. 5 (October 13, 2009): 519.

[80] Paul Slovic, "Iconic Photographs and the Ebb and Flow of Empathic Response to Humanitarian Disasters," *Proceedings of the National Academy of Sciences* 114, no. 8 (January 24, 2017): 640–44.

[81] Ibid.

[82] Julissa Higgins, "Read George W. Bush's Speech on the Dallas Shooting," *Time*, July 12, 2016, http://time.com/4403510/george-w-bush-speech-dallas-shooting-memorial-service.

[83] Volf, *Exclusion and Embrace*, 100.

Chapter 9

84 U.S. Census Bureau, "QuickFacts: Mississippi," https://www.census.gov/quickfacts/MS.

85 U.S. Census Bureau, "Mississippi: 2000," August 2002, https://www.census.gov/prod/2002pubs/c2kprof00-ms.pdf

86 U.S. Census Bureau, "QuickFacts: Mississippi."

87 Alister E. McGrath, *Mere Apologetics: How to Help Seekers and Skeptics Find Faith* (Seoul: DMI Press, 2014), 45.